Interactive Notebooks

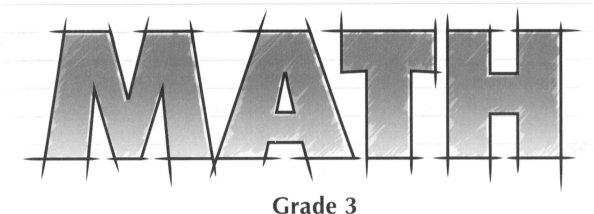

Grade 3

Credits

Content Editor: Elise Craver

Visit *carsondellosa.com* for correlations to Common Core, state, national, and Canadian provincial standards.

Carson-Dellosa Publishing, LLC
PO Box 35665
Greensboro, NC 27425 USA
carsondellosa.com

978-1-4838-2479-6
05-128177784

Table of Contents

Number and Operations in Base Ten

Operations and Algebraic Thinking

Number and Operations—Fractions

Measurement and Data

Geometry

Reproducibles

What Are Interactive Notebooks?

Interactive notebooks are a unique form of note taking. Teachers guide students through creating pages of notes on new topics. Instead of being in the traditional linear, handwritten format, notes are colorful and spread across the pages. Notes also often include drawings, diagrams, and 3-D elements to make the material understandable and relevant. Students are encouraged to complete their notebook pages in ways that make sense to them. With this personalization, no two pages are exactly the same.

Because of their creative nature, interactive notebooks allow students to be active participants in their own learning. Teachers can easily differentiate pages to address the levels and needs of each learner. The notebooks are arranged sequentially, and students can create tables of contents as they create pages, making it simple for students to use their notebooks for reference throughout the year. The interactive, easily personalized format makes interactive notebooks ideal for engaging students in learning new concepts.

Using interactive notebooks can take as much or as little time as you like. Students will initially take longer to create pages but will get faster as they become familiar with the process of creating pages. You may choose to only create a notebook page as a class at the beginning of each unit, or you may choose to create a new page for each topic within a unit. You can decide what works best for your students and schedule.

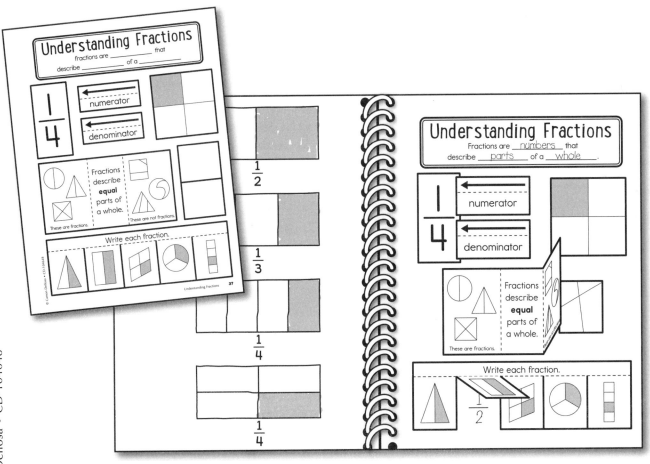

A student's interactive notebook for a fractions page

Getting Started

You can start using interactive notebooks at any point in the school year. Use the following guidelines to help you get started in your classroom. (For more specific details, management ideas, and tips, see page 10.)

1. **Plan each notebook.**

   Use the planning template (page 9) to lay out a general plan for the topics you plan to cover in each notebook for the year.

2. **Choose a notebook type.**

   Interactive notebooks are usually either single-subject, spiral-bound notebooks, composition books, or three-ring binders with loose-leaf paper. Each type presents pros and cons. See page 5 for a more in-depth look at each type of notebook.

3. **Allow students to personalize their notebooks.**

   Have students decorate their notebook covers, as well as add their names and subjects. This provides a sense of ownership and emphasizes the personalized nature of the notebooks.

4. **Number the pages and create the table of contents.**

   Have students number the bottom outside corner of each page, front and back. When completing a new page, adding a table of contents entry will be easy. Have students title the first page of each notebook "Table of Contents." Have them leave several blank pages at the front of each notebook for the table of contents. Refer to your general plan for an idea of about how many entries students will be creating.

5. **Start creating pages.**

   Always begin a new page by adding an entry to the table of contents. Create the first notebook pages along with students to model proper format and expectations.

This book contains individual topics for you to introduce. Use the pages in the order that best fits your curriculum. You may also choose to alter the content presented to better match your school's curriculum. The provided lesson plans often do not instruct students to add color. Students should make their own choices about personalizing the content in a way that makes sense to them. Encourage students to highlight and color the pages as they desire while creating them.

After introducing topics, you may choose to add more practice pages. Use the reproducibles (pages 78–96) to easily create new notebook pages for practice or to introduce topics not addressed in this book.

Use the grading rubric (page 11) to grade students' interactive notebooks at various points throughout the year. Provide students copies of the rubric to glue into their notebooks and refer to as they create pages.

What Type of Notebook Should I Use?

Spiral Notebook

The pages in this book are formatted for a standard one-subject notebook.

Pros

- Notebook can be folded in half.
- Page size is larger.
- It is inexpensive.
- It often comes with pockets for storing materials.

Cons

- Pages can easily fall out.
- Spirals can snag or become misshapen.
- Page count and size vary widely.
- It is not as durable as a binder.

Tips

- Encase the spiral in duct tape to make it more durable.
- Keep the notebooks in a central place to prevent them from getting damaged in desks.

Composition Notebook

Pros

- Pages don't easily fall out.
- Page size and page count are standard.
- It is inexpensive.

Cons

- Notebook cannot be folded in half.
- Page size is smaller.
- It is not as durable as a binder.

Tips

- Copy pages meant for standard-sized notebooks at 85 or 90 percent. Test to see which works better for your notebook.

Binder with Loose-Leaf Paper

Pros

- Pages can be easily added, moved, or removed.
- Pages can be removed individually for grading.
- You can add full-page printed handouts.
- It has durable covers.

Cons

- Pages can easily fall out.
- Pages aren't durable.
- It is more expensive than a notebook.
- Students can easily misplace or lose pages.
- Larger size makes it more difficult to store.

Tips

- Provide hole reinforcers for damaged pages.

How to Organize an Interactive Notebook

You may organize an interactive notebook in many different ways. You may choose to organize it by unit and work sequentially through the book. Or, you may choose to create different sections that you will revisit and add to throughout the year. Choose the format that works best for your students and subject.

An interactive notebook includes different types of pages in addition to the pages students create. Non-content pages you may want to add include the following:

Title Page

This page is useful for quickly identifying notebooks. It is especially helpful in classrooms that use multiple interactive notebooks for different subjects. Have students write the subject (such as "Math") on the title page of each interactive notebook. They should also include their full names. You may choose to have them include other information such as the teacher's name, classroom number, or class period.

Table of Contents

The table of contents is an integral part of the interactive notebook. It makes referencing previously created pages quick and easy for students. Make sure that students leave several pages at the beginning of each notebook for a table of contents.

Expectations and Grading Rubric

It is helpful for each student to have a copy of the expectations for creating interactive notebook pages. You may choose to include a list of expectations for parents and students to sign, as well as a grading rubric (page 11).

Unit Title Pages

Consider using a single page at the beginning of each section to separate it. Title the page with the unit name. Add a tab (page 78) to the edge of the page to make it easy to flip to the unit. Add a table of contents for only the pages in that unit.

Glossary

Reserve a six-page section at the back of the notebook where students can create a glossary. Draw a line to split in half the front and back of each page, creating 24 sections. Combine Q and R and Y and Z to fit the entire alphabet. Have students add an entry as each new vocabulary word is introduced.

Formatting Student Notebook Pages

The other major consideration for planning an interactive notebook is how to treat the left and right sides of a notebook spread. Interactive journals are usually viewed with the notebook open flat. This creates a left side and a right side. You have several options for how to treat the two sides of the spread.

Traditionally, the right side is used for the teacher-directed part of the lesson, and the left side is used for students to interact with the lesson content. The lessons in this book use this format. However, you may prefer to switch the order for your class so that the teacher-directed learning is on the left and the student input is on the right.

It can also be important to include standards, learning objectives, or essential questions in interactive notebooks. You may choose to write these on the top-left side of each page before completing the teacher-directed page on the right side. You may also choose to have students include the "Introduction" part of each lesson in that same top-left section. This is the *in, through, out* method. Students enter *in* the lesson on the top left of the page, go *through* the lesson on the right page, and exit *out* of the lesson on the bottom left with a reflection activity.

The following chart details different types of items and activities that you could include on each side.

Left Side Student Output	Right Side Teacher-Directed Learning
• learning objectives • essential questions • I Can statements • brainstorming • making connections • summarizing • making conclusions • practice problems • opinions • questions • mnemonics • drawings and diagrams	• vocabulary and definitions • mini-lessons • folding activities • steps in a process • example problems • notes • diagrams • graphic organizers • hints and tips • big ideas

Planning for the Year

Making a general plan for interactive notebooks will help with planning, grading, and testing throughout the year. You do not need to plan every single page, but knowing what topics you will cover and in what order can be helpful in many ways.

Use the Interactive Notebook Plan (page 9) to plan your units and topics and where they should be placed in the notebooks. Remember to include enough pages at the beginning for the non-content pages, such as the title page, table of contents, and grading rubric. You may also want to leave a page at the beginning of each unit to place a mini table of contents for just that section.

In addition, when planning new pages, it can be helpful to sketch the pieces you will need to create. Use the following notebook template and notes to plan new pages.

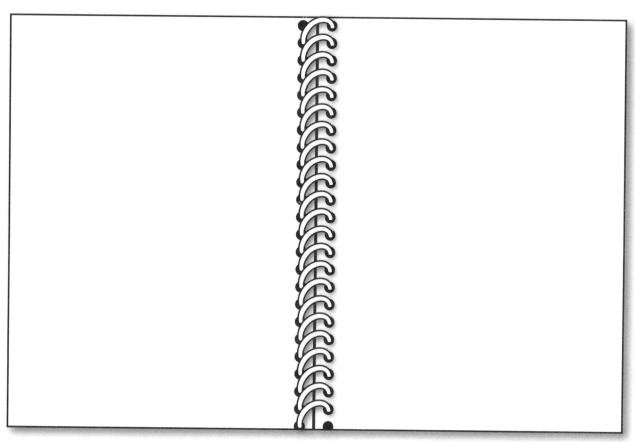

Left Side   **Right Side**

Notes

_____

_____

_____

Interactive Notebook Plan

Page	Topic	Page	Topic
1		51	
2		52	
3		53	
4		54	
5		55	
6		56	
7		57	
8		58	
9		59	
10		60	
11		61	
12		62	
13		63	
14		64	
15		65	
16		66	
17		67	
18		68	
19		69	
20		70	
21		71	
22		72	
23		73	
24		74	
25		75	
26		76	
27		77	
28		78	
29		79	
30		80	
31		81	
32		82	
33		83	
34		84	
35		85	
36		86	
37		87	
38		88	
39		89	
40		90	
41		91	
42		92	
43		93	
44		94	
45		95	
46		96	
47		97	
48		98	
49		99	
50		100	

Managing Interactive Notebooks in the Classroom

Working with Younger Students

- Use your yearly plan to preprogram a table of contents that you can copy and give to students to glue into their notebooks, instead of writing individual entries.

- Have assistants or parent volunteers precut pieces.

- Create glue sponges to make gluing easier. Place large sponges in plastic containers with white glue. The sponges will absorb the glue. Students can wipe the backs of pieces across the sponges to apply the glue with less mess.

Creating Notebook Pages

- For storing loose pieces, add a pocket to the inside back cover. Use the envelope pattern (page 81), an envelope, or a resealable plastic bag. Or, tape the bottom and side edges of the two last pages of the notebook together to create a large pocket.

- When writing under flaps, have students trace the outline of each flap so that they can visualize the writing boundary.

- Where the dashed line will be hidden on the inside of the fold, have students first fold the piece in the opposite direction so that they can see the dashed line. Then, students should fold the piece back the other way along the same fold line to create the fold in the correct direction.

- To avoid losing pieces, have students keep all of their scraps on their desks until they have finished each page.

- To contain paper scraps and avoid multiple trips to the trash can, provide small groups with small buckets or tubs.

- For students who run out of room, keep full and half sheets available. Students can glue these to the bottom of the pages and fold them up when not in use.

Dealing with Absences

- Create a model notebook for absent students to reference when they return to school.

- Have students cut a second set of pieces as they work on their own pages.

Using the Notebook

- To organize sections of the notebook, provide each student with a sheet of tabs (page 78).

- To easily find the next blank page, either cut off the top-right corner of each page as it is used or attach a long piece of yarn or ribbon to the back cover to be used as a bookmark.

Interactive Notebook Grading Rubric

4

_____ Table of contents is complete.

_____ All notebook pages are included.

_____ All notebook pages are complete.

_____ Notebook pages are neat and organized.

_____ Information is correct.

_____ Pages show personalization, evidence of learning, and original ideas.

3

_____ Table of contents is mostly complete.

_____ One notebook page is missing.

_____ Notebook pages are mostly complete.

_____ Notebook pages are mostly neat and organized.

_____ Information is mostly correct.

_____ Pages show some personalization, evidence of learning, and original ideas.

2

_____ Table of contents is missing a few entries.

_____ A few notebook pages are missing.

_____ A few notebook pages are incomplete.

_____ Notebook pages are somewhat messy and unorganized.

_____ Information has several errors.

_____ Pages show little personalization, evidence of learning, or original ideas.

1

_____ Table of contents is incomplete.

_____ Many notebook pages are missing.

_____ Many notebook pages are incomplete.

_____ Notebook pages are too messy and unorganized to use.

_____ Information is incorrect.

_____ Pages show no personalization, evidence of learning, or original ideas.

Place Value

Introduction

Review simple place value. Write three digits on the board such as 4, 8, and 2. Challenge students to use the digits to write the smallest number they can. Then, have students use the same digits to write the greatest number they can. Have students explain how they knew the best order to arrange the digits to form the smallest and greatest numbers.

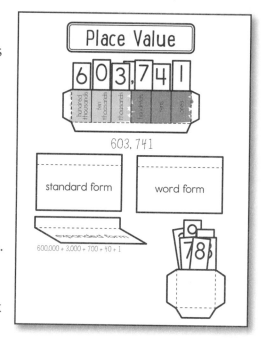

Creating the Notebook Page

Guide students through the following steps to complete the right-hand page in their notebooks.

1. Add a Table of Contents entry for the Place Value pages.

2. Cut out the title and glue it to the top of the page.

3. Cut out the piece with six boxes. Apply glue to the back of the tabs and attach it below the title, leaving space above it.

4. Label each box with the place values from *ones* to *hundred thousands*. Color the hundreds period one color and the thousands period a different color.

5. Cut out the pocket. Apply glue to the back of the tabs and attach it to the bottom of the page.

6. Cut out the number and comma pieces. Store them in the pocket created in step 5.

7. Say values such as *7 hundreds, 3 thousands*, etc. Place the number cards in the place value pocket to create a six-digit number with the matching values. Record the number on the page below the pocket.

8. Cut out the three *form* flaps. Apply glue to the back of the top sections and attach them to the bottom of the page.

9. Under each flap, write the correct form of the number written above.

Reflect on Learning

To complete the left-hand page, have students explain how many total hundreds are in the following numbers: 3,400; 45,000; 1,200; and 67,550. For example, *there are 15 hundreds in 1,500.*

Place Value

0	3	6	9	9
0	3	6	9	9
1	4	7	,	,
1	4	7		
2	5	8		
2	5	8		

standard form

word form

expanded form

Rounding Numbers

Have students pretend they are planning a festival. Last year, 689 people attended the festival. Ask students how many T-shirts they think need to be ordered. How many hot dogs do they need to buy? How many drinks? Write the answers on the board and discuss the numbers. Were they specific numbers like 689 or more rounded numbers like 700? Why?

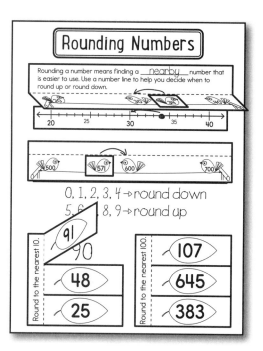

Creating the Notebook Page

Guide students through the following steps to complete the right-hand page in their notebooks.

1. Add a Table of Contents entry for the Rounding Numbers pages.

2. Cut out the title and glue it to the top of the page.

3. Cut out the *Rounding a number* flap. Apply glue to the back of the top section and attach it below the title.

4. Discuss what it means to round a number. Complete the sentence. (Rounding a number means finding a **nearby** number that is easier to use.) Discuss scenarios when it would be helpful to round numbers.

5. Cut out the *20, 30, 40* number line and glue it under the flap.

6. Cut out the *34* bird. Glue it in the correct place on top of the flap. Lift the flap and draw a dot where 34 is on the number line. Decide which ten 34 is closest to, 30 or 40. Draw arrows on the flap and the number line to show which number 34 should round to.

7. Repeat step 3 with the *500, 600, 700* flap and repeat steps 5 and 6 with the *500, 600, 700* number line and the *571* bird.

8. Discuss the rules for rounding numbers. Write the rules on the page below the *500, 600, 700* flap.

9. Cut out the flap books. Cut on the solid lines to create three flaps on each book. Apply glue to the back of the left sections and attach them to the bottom of the page.

10. Follow the directions on each flap book. Write the rounded number under each flap.

Reflect on Learning

To complete the left-hand page, have students describe how they think they would round a number to the nearest thousand. Write the number 1,232 on the board. Have students use number lines or other methods to describe how to round it to the nearest thousand.

Rounding Numbers

Rounding a number means finding a _____ number that is easier to use. Use a number line to help you decide when to round up or round down.

  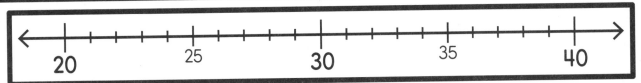

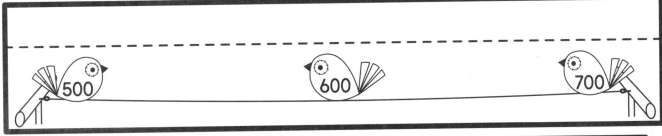

20   25   30   35   40

500   550   600   650   700

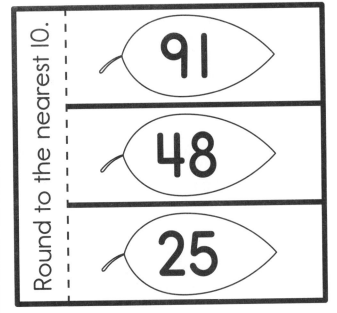

Round to the nearest 10.

91

48

25

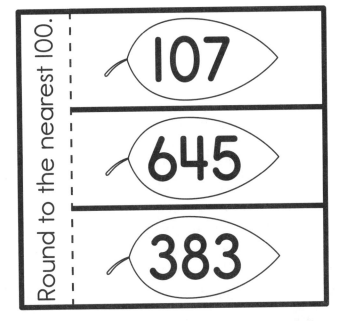

Round to the nearest 100.

107

645

383

Comparing and Ordering Numbers

Introduction

Review place value. Say different values and have students build the numbers. For example, if you say *4 tens, 2 thousands, 7 ones, and 9 hundreds*, students should write 2,947. Repeat several times. Then, have students find the numbers in their lists with the greatest number of ones, the greatest number of tens, etc.

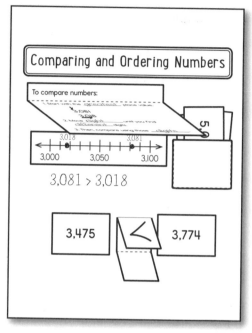

Creating the Notebook Page

Guide students through the following steps to complete the right-hand page in their notebooks.

1. Add a Table of Contents entry for the Comparing and Ordering Numbers pages.

2. Cut out the title and glue it to the top of the page.

3. Cut out the flap. Apply glue to the back of the top section and attach it to the top left of the page.

4. Complete the steps on the flap by filling in the blanks. (1. Start with the **greatest** place value. 2. Move **right** until you find **different** digits. 3. Then, compare using those **digits**.)

5. Cut out the number line and glue it under the flap.

6. Mark the example numbers from the flap on the number line. Write a true comparison sentence with the numbers (3,081 > 3,018).

7. Cut out the piece with the equal sign. Apply glue to the back of the middle section. Attach it to the center of the bottom half of the page so that the flaps open up and down.

8. Flip down the top flap and draw a less than symbol (<) on it. Flip up the bottom flap and draw a greater than symbol (>) on it.

9. Cut out the pocket. Apply glue to the back of the tabs and attach it to the page beside the *To compare numbers* piece.

10. Cut out the number cards. Place one card on each side of the symbols piece. Unfold the flaps to create a true number comparison. Or, choose three or more cards to place in order from least to greatest or greatest to least. For more practice, write additional numbers on the backs of the cards. Store the cards in the pocket when not in use.

Reflect on Learning

To complete the left-hand page, have students write all six numbers from the right-hand page in order from least to greatest. Then, students should add a number that would belong between the two middle numbers.

Comparing and Ordering Numbers

7,345	7,453	3,475
5,734	5,034	3,774

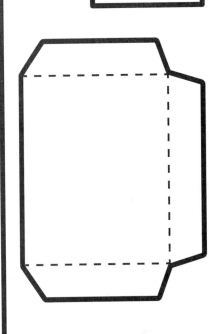

To compare numbers:

1. Start with the _____ place value.

→ 3,081
→ 3,018

2. Move _____ until you find _____ digits.

3. Then, compare using those _____.

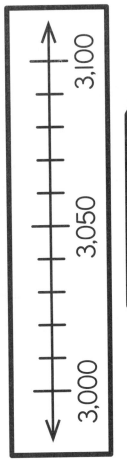

3,100

3,050

3,000

Adding and Subtracting within 1,000

Introduction

Review regrouping and borrowing. Provide pairs of students with sets of base ten blocks. Have each pair start with a hundreds flat. Write the problem *100 – 78* on the board and have students borrow from the hundreds flat to solve the problem. Next, have students start with four tens rods and six ones cubes. Write the problem *46 + 39* on the board and have students regroup by exchanging their ones cubes for a tens rod to solve the problem.

Creating the Notebook Page

Guide students through the following steps to complete the right-hand page in their notebooks.

1. Add a Table of Contents entry for the Adding and Subtracting within 1,000 pages.

2. Cut out the title and glue it to the top of the page.

3. Cut out the base ten blocks key and glue it below the title.

4. Cut out the trifold pieces. With the blank sides faceup, fold the top and bottom sections on the dashed lines so that the small pieces overlap the large pieces. Apply glue to the gray glue sections and attach them to the page.

5. Solve each problem. Write the answer on the small flap. Inside each trifold piece, draw base ten blocks to show the borrowing or regrouping done in the problem.

Reflect on Learning

To complete the left-hand page, have students choose one of the addition problems and one of the subtraction problems from the right-hand side of the page. Students should explain or show the strategies they used to solve each problem.

Answer Key

856 + 171 = 1,027; 438 + 366 = 804; 527 – 404 = 123; 780 – 639 = 141

Adding and Subtracting within 1,000

glue

856
+ 171

glue

438
+ 366

glue

527
− 404

glue

780
− 639

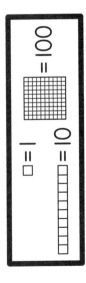

□ = 1
▭ = 10
▦ = 100

Understanding Multiplication

Review arrays. Provide students with manipulatives such as counters or tiles. Write a repeated addition sentence on the board and have students model and solve it with an array. Then, have students create arrays and share the related addition sentences.

Creating the Notebook Page

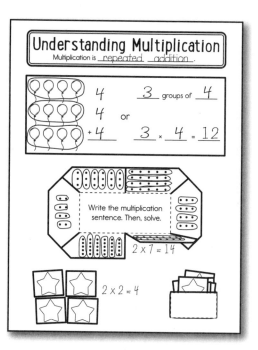

Guide students through the following steps to complete the right-hand page in their notebooks.

1. Add a Table of Contents entry for the Understanding Multiplication pages.

2. Cut out the title and glue it to the top of the page.

3. Complete the definition of *multiplication*. (Multiplication is **repeated addition**.)

4. Cut out the balloon piece and glue it below the title.

5. Look at the balloons and discuss different ways to group them evenly. Draw circles around the rows to create three groups of four. To the right of each row, write the total number of balloons. Then, write the sum for the addition sentence. Discuss how the grouping and repeated addition translate into a multiplication sentence. Complete the number sentences (**3** groups of **4, 3 × 4 = 12**).

6. Cut out the array flap book. Cut on the solid lines to create six flaps. Apply glue to the back of the center section and place it below the balloon piece.

7. On each flap, draw circles to show equal groups. Under each flap, write the related multiplication sentence and solve it.

8. Cut out the pocket. Apply glue to the back of the tabs and attach it to the bottom right of the page.

9. Cut out the stars. Use the stars to create different arrays. Write a multiplication sentence for each array on the page and solve it. Store the stars in the pocket when not in use.

Reflect on Learning

To complete the left-hand page, display a non-square array (such as a 4 by 7 array or a 3 by 8 array) on the board. Have students explain two different ways to solve the array and write the related multiplication sentence for each way. Students should describe why the two multiplication sentences are related.

Understanding Multiplication

Multiplication is _____ _____ .

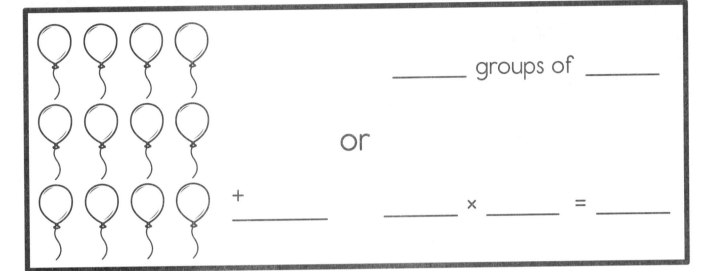

_____ groups of _____

or

+ _____

_____ × _____ = _____

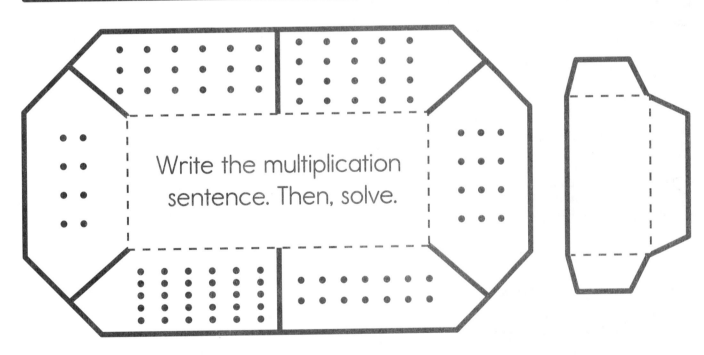

Write the multiplication sentence. Then, solve.

Multiplication

Introduction

Practice counting by multiples. As a class, count aloud by 2s, 5s, and 10s. Then, challenge students to count by more challenging multiples such as 3s or 4s. Explain that counting by multiples is also multiplying and can be used as a strategy to find products.

Creating the Notebook Page

Guide students through the following steps to complete the right-hand page in their notebooks.

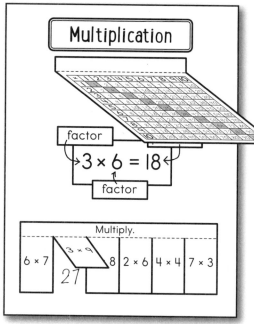

1. Add a Table of Contents entry for the Multiplication pages.

2. Cut out the title and glue it to the top of the page.

3. Cut out the multiplication chart. Apply glue to the back of the top section and attach it below the title.

4. Complete the multiplication chart. Look at the patterns, including the grayed-out square numbers. Discuss how patterns can be helpful when memorizing multiplication tables.

5. Cut out the *3 x 6 = 18* piece and glue it under the multiplication chart. Cut out the *factor* and *product* labels.

6. Discuss the parts of a multiplication problem. Glue the labels to the multiplication problem to label each part.

7. Cut out the flap book. Cut on the solid lines to create six flaps. Apply glue to the back of the top section and attach it to the bottom of the page.

8. Solve each multiplication problem. Write the answer under each flap.

Reflect on Learning

To complete the left-hand page, have students look for patterns in the multiplication table on the right-hand page. Students should describe any patterns they find in their own words and explain how the patterns may help them solve related multiplication problems.

© Carson-Dellosa • CD-104648

Multiplication

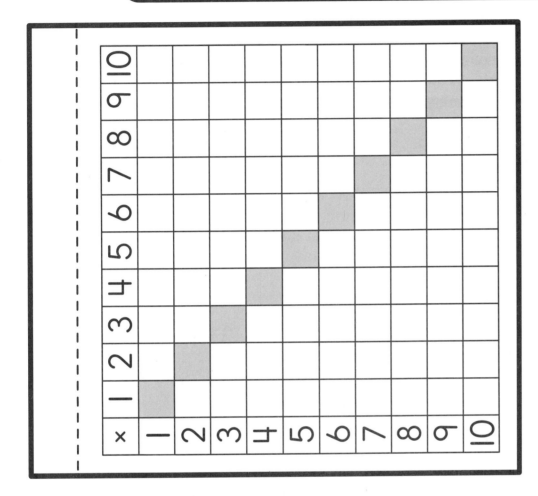

$$3 \times 6 = 18$$

| factor | factor | product |

Multiply.

| 6×7 | 3×9 | 5×8 | 2×6 | 4×4 | 7×3 |

Multiplying by Multiples of 10

Introduction

Provide students with 10 base ten rods. Ask students to show two of the tens rods and tell how many they represent (20). Repeat with three (30), four (40), five (50), etc. Have students refer to a multiplication chart and look at the ×10 column. As a class, discuss any patterns students noticed in the amount of tens rods and in the the multiplication chart.

Multiplying by Multiples of 10

$3 \times 2 = 6$

The 6 stays the same. You just add a zero. It's like you are counting by 10s. You can just multiply the numbers and add a zero to the end.

If $4 \times 6 = 24$, then $4 \times 60 = $ 240

If $7 \times 5 = 35$, then $7 \times 50 = $

$6 \times 70 = 420$

$3 \times 80 = 240$

$5 \times 50 = 250$

$4 \times 20 = 80$

$1 \times 20 = $ 3   40

Creating the Notebook Page

Guide students through the following steps to complete the right-hand page in their notebooks.

1. Add a Table of Contents entry for the Multiplying by Multiples of 10 pages.

2. Cut out the title and glue it to the top of the page.

3. Cut out the $3 \times 20 = $ piece. Fold the blank section on the dashed line so that it covers the 0 in the 20. Apply glue to the back of the left section and attach it to the left side of the page below the title.

4. Keeping the piece folded, look at the base ten blocks and solve the problem 3×2. Write the answer on the flap (**= 6**). Then, open the flap. Look at the new problem and base ten blocks. Solve the new problem and write the answer on the line (**60**). Discuss any patterns you notice and similarities in the answers. Write your observations on the page to the right of the piece.

5. Cut out the two flaps. Apply glue to the back of the left sections and attach them side by side in the middle of the page.

6. Read the problem on each flap and write the answer under the flap.

7. Cut out the x, = piece. Cut on the solid lines to create two flaps. Cut out the two number strips. Slide the number strips over the center flaps on the x, = piece so that the single digits show to the left of the multiplication sign and the multiples of 10 show to the right. Keeping the strips in place, flip the piece facedown. Apply glue to the center, left, and right sections. Do not apply glue to the number strips. Flip the piece back over and attach it to the bottom of the page.

8. Slide the number strips to create different multiplication problems. Write each problem on the page around the slider and solve it.

Reflect on Learning

To complete the left-hand page, have students write a rule for multiplying a single-digit number by a multiple of 10. Students should provide several examples to prove that their rule works.

Multiplying by Multiples of 10

$3 \times 20 = $ ____

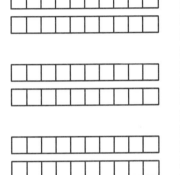

If $4 \times 6 = 24$, then $4 \times 60 = $

If $7 \times 5 = 35$, then $7 \times 50 = $

1	10
2	20
3	30
4	40
5	50
6	60
7	70
8	80
9	90

____ × ____ = ____

Multiplying by Two-Digit Numbers

Divide students into pairs. Give each pair a set of multiplication flash cards. Have each student test his partner on several multiplication facts. Then, have students switch roles and repeat.

Creating the Notebook Page

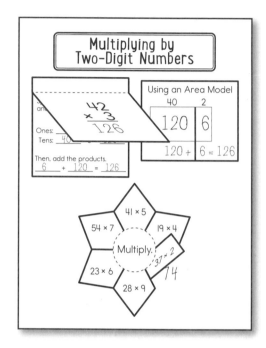

Guide students through the following steps to complete the right-hand page in their notebooks.

1. Add a Table of Contents entry for the Multiplying by Two-Digit Numbers pages.

2. Cut out the title and glue it to the top of the page.

3. Cut out the *42 × 3* and the *Split the problem* flaps. Apply glue to the gray glue section and place the *42 × 3* flap on top to create a two-flap book. Apply glue to the back of the top section and attach it to the left side of the page below the title.

4. Lift the flap and discuss how to break apart a more complex multiplication problem. Follow the steps to complete the problem (**2 × 3 = 6**; **40 × 3 = 120**; **6 + 120 = 126**). Then, do the same on the top flap. Discuss how to "regroup" when the product of the ones is greater than 10. Write an example under the flap.

5. Cut out the *Using an Area Model* piece. Cut on the solid line to create two flaps. Apply glue to the back of the top section and attach it to the right of the *42 × 3* flap.

6. Solve each section of the area model on top of the flaps. Under each flap, write the related part of the multiplication problem. Discuss how all three methods for solving the same problem ended with the same product.

7. Cut out the *Multiply* flower. Cut on the solid lines to create six flaps. Apply glue to the back of the center section and attach it to the bottom of the page.

8. Solve each problem. Write the answer under the flap.

Reflect on Learning

To complete the left-hand page, have students describe how carrying from the ones to the tens in multiplication is similar to and different from carrying in addition.

Answer Key
Clockwise from the top: 205; 76; 74; 252; 138; 378

Multiplying by Two-Digit Numbers

$$42$$
$$\times\ 3$$

Split the problem into ones and tens.

$$42 \times 3$$

Ones: _____ × 3 = _____

Tens: _____ × 3 = _____

Then, add the products.

_____ + _____ = _____

Using an Area Model

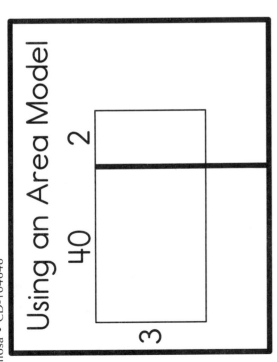

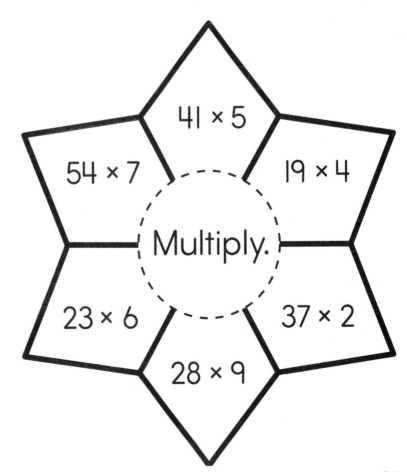

Multiply.

41 × 5

54 × 7

19 × 4

23 × 6

37 × 2

28 × 9

Understanding Division

Introduction

Divide students into pairs. Provide each pair with 10 manipulatives such as counters, base ten blocks, or buttons. Have each pair take two of the objects and decide how to divide the objects evenly between them. Discuss how they knew how to divide two objects between two people. Repeat with four objects. Finally, repeat with 10 objects.

Creating the Notebook Page

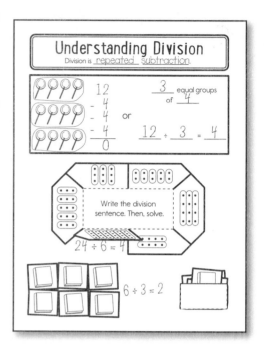

Guide students through the following steps to complete the right-hand page in their notebooks.

1. Add a Table of Contents entry for the Understanding Division pages.

2. Cut out the title and glue it to the top of the page.

3. Complete the definition of *division*. (Division is **repeated subtraction**.)

4. Cut out the lollipop piece and glue it below the title.

5. Look at the lollipops and discuss different ways to divide them evenly. Draw circles around the rows to create three groups of four. To the right of the top row, write the total number of lollipops. Then, write the number of lollipops subtracted from each row. Discuss how the grouping and repeated subtraction translate into a division sentence. Complete the number sentences (**3** equal groups of **4, 12 ÷ 3 = 4**).

6. Cut out the array flap book. Cut on the solid lines to create six flaps. Apply glue to the back of the center section and place it below the lollipop piece.

7. On each flap, look at the equal groups. Under each flap, write the related division sentence and solve it.

8. Cut out the pocket. Apply glue to the back of each tab and attach it to the bottom right of the page.

9. Cut out the books. Use the books to create different arrays. Write a division sentence for each array on the page and solve it. Store the books in the pocket when not in use.

Reflect on Learning

To complete the left-hand page, display an array. Have students copy the array and write the two possible related division sentences.

Understanding Division

Division is _____ _____.

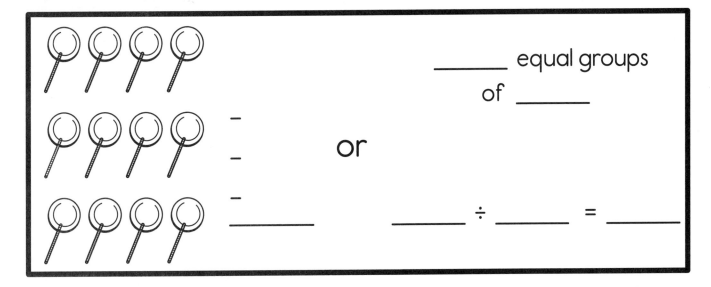

_____ equal groups

of _____

or

_____ ÷ _____ = _____

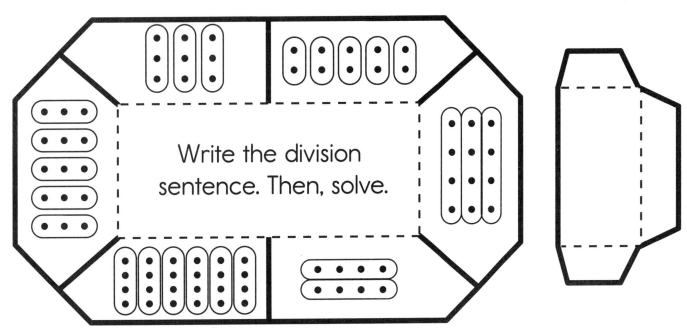

Write the division sentence. Then, solve.

Properties of Operations

Introduction

Write the problem *5 + 6* on the board. Have a student solve it. Then, write the problem *6 + 5* on the board. Have a different student solve it. As a class, discuss why the sums for the two different problems were the same. Explain that multiplication problems have similar properties.

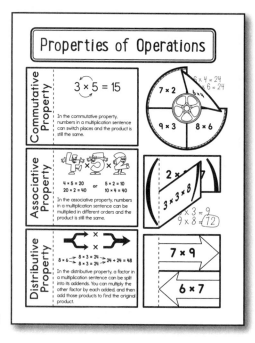

Creating the Notebook Page

Guide students through the following steps to complete the right-hand page in their notebooks.

1. Add a Table of Contents entry for the Properties of Operations pages.

2. Cut out the title and glue it to the top of the page.

3. Cut out the three *Property* flaps. Apply glue to the back of the left sections and attach them along the left side of the page.

4. Read each flap. Discuss how the diagram on each flap reflects the property shown. Under the flap, give a different example to show how that property works.

5. Cut out the tire flap piece. Cut on the solid lines to create four flaps. Apply glue to the back of the center section and attach it to the right of the *Commutative Property* flap.

6. Cut out the brackets and arrows flap pieces. Cut on the solid lines to create two flaps on each piece. Apply glue to the back of the left section of each piece. Attach the brackets piece to the right of the *Associative Property* flap. Attach the arrows piece to the right of the *Distributive Property* flap.

7. Discuss how the art on each flap book relates to the property it represents. Then, rewrite each problem under the flap to show the property in use and solve.

Reflect on Learning

To complete the left-hand page, have students describe how the properties of operations can help solve problems such as $4 \times ? \times 2 = 24$.

Properties of Operations

Commutative Property

$3 \times 5 = 15$

In the commutative property, numbers in a multiplication sentence can switch places, and the product is still the same.

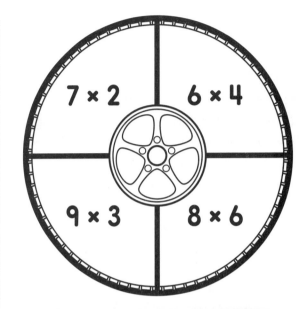

7 × 2   6 × 4

9 × 3   8 × 6

Associative Property

$4 \times 5 = 20$
$20 \times 2 = 40$
or
$5 \times 2 = 10$
$10 \times 4 = 40$

In the associative property, numbers in a multiplication sentence can be multiplied in different orders, and the product is still the same.

Distributive Property

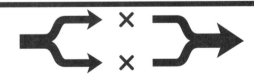

8×6
$8 \times 3 = 24$
$8 \times 3 = 24$
$24 + 24 = 48$

In the distributive property, a factor in a multiplication sentence can be split into its addends. You can multiply the other factor by each added and then add those products to find the original product.

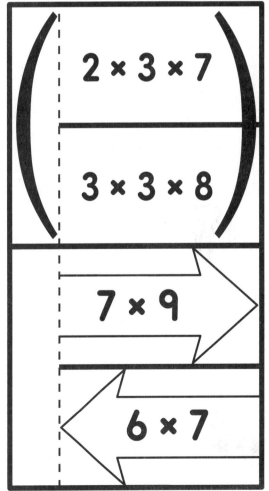

$2 \times 3 \times 7$

$3 \times 3 \times 8$

7×9

6×7

Identifying Patterns

Introduction

Display a pattern on the board, such as *circle, circle, triangle, circle, circle, triangle,* or *2, 4, 6, 8*. Have students identify, extend, and explain the patterns. Explain that mathematicians train their brains to look for patterns to better solve problems and learn about numbers.

Creating the Notebook Page

Guide students through the following steps to complete the right-hand page in their notebooks.

1. Add a Table of Contents entry for the Identifying Patterns pages.

2. Cut out the title and glue it to the top of the page.

3. Cut out the *For each chart* piece and glue it to the left-hand side of the page below the title.

4. Cut out the three flaps. Apply glue to the back of the top sections and attach each flap to the page.

5. Follow the directions on the *For each chart* piece to complete each flap.

Reflect on Learning

To complete the left-hand page, have students choose one of the patterns they explored on the right-hand page and explain how they could use it to help solve other math problems.

Identifying Patterns

For each chart, choose a rule from below or make up your own. Write the rule at the top of the chart. Follow the rule and color the numbers on the chart. Look for patterns. Under the flap, describe the patterns you see and explain them using the properties of operations.

- add an even number and an odd number
- add two even numbers
- add two odd numbers
- multiply a number by itself
- add 9
- multiply by 3

Rule:

1	2	3	4	5	6	7	8	9	10
11	12	13	14	15	16	17	18	19	20
21	22	23	24	25	26	27	28	29	30
31	32	33	34	35	36	37	38	39	40
41	42	43	44	45	46	47	48	49	50
51	52	53	54	55	56	57	58	59	60
61	62	63	64	65	66	67	68	69	70
71	72	73	74	75	76	77	78	79	80
81	82	83	84	85	86	87	88	89	90
91	92	93	94	95	96	97	98	99	100

Rule:

+	1	2	3	4	5	6	7	8	9
1	2	3	4	5	6	7	8	9	10
2	3	4	5	6	7	8	9	10	11
3	4	5	6	7	8	9	10	11	12
4	5	6	7	8	9	10	11	12	13
5	6	7	8	9	10	11	12	13	14
6	7	8	9	10	11	12	13	14	15
7	8	9	10	11	12	13	14	15	16
8	9	10	11	12	13	14	15	16	17
9	10	11	12	13	14	15	16	17	18

Rule:

×	1	2	3	4	5	6	7	8	9
1	1	2	3	4	5	6	7	8	9
2	2	4	6	8	10	12	14	16	18
3	3	6	9	12	15	18	21	24	27
4	4	8	12	16	20	24	28	32	36
5	5	10	15	20	25	30	35	40	45
6	6	12	18	24	30	36	42	48	54
7	7	14	21	28	35	42	49	56	63
8	8	16	24	32	40	48	56	64	72
9	9	18	27	36	45	54	63	72	81

Unknown Numbers

Introduction

Write the following equations on the board: *8 + ? = 20, ? – 5 = 5,* and *? + 4 = 12*. Have students find the missing number in each equation. Allow students to share their answers. As a class, discuss the different strategies students used to find the missing numbers in each equation.

Creating the Notebook Page

Guide students through the following steps to complete the right-hand page in their notebooks.

1. Add a Table of Contents entry for the Unknown Numbers pages.

2. Cut out the title and glue it to the top of the page.

3. Cut out the *Someone got paint* piece and glue it below the title.

4. Cut out the paint cans. Apply glue to the back of the top sections and attach them to the bottom of the page.

5. Follow the directions on the *Someone got paint* piece to complete each flap and show your understanding of the relationship between multiplication and division. Write the missing number on the top of each flap.

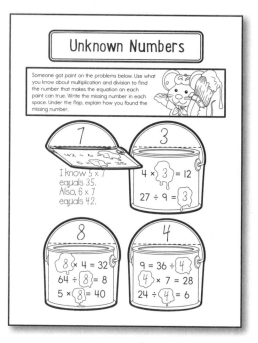

Reflect on Learning

To complete the left-hand page, have students explain the relationship between multiplication and division in their own words. Then, have students draw pictures to illustrate their explanations.

Answer Key

7; 3; 8; 4

Unknown Numbers

© Carson-Dellosa • CD-104648

Someone got paint on the problems below. Use what you know about multiplication and division to find the number that makes the equation on each paint can true. Write the missing number in each space. Under the flap, explain how you found the missing number.

$$42 \div 6 = $$

$$5 \times = 35$$

$$4 \times = 12$$

$$27 \div 9 = $$

$$ \times 4 = 32$$

$$64 \div = 8$$

$$5 \times = 40$$

$$9 = 36 \div $$

$$ \times 7 = 28$$

$$24 \div = 6$$

Understanding Fractions

Introduction

Review partitioning. Provide each student with two blank index cards. Have students partition one side of a card into two equal parts and the other side into three equal parts. They should partition the remaining card into four equal parts in a different way on each side. Emphasize how the divisions must be equal.

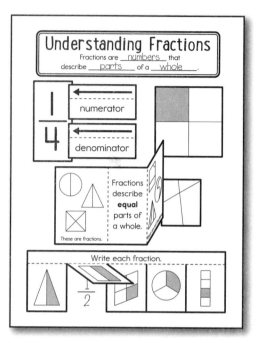

Creating the Notebook Page

Guide students through the following steps to complete the right-hand page in their notebooks.

1. Add a Table of Contents entry for the Understanding Fractions pages.

2. Cut out the title and glue it to the top of the page.

3. Complete the definition for *fractions*. (Fractions are **numbers** that describe **parts** of a **whole**.)

4. Cut out the $\frac{1}{4}$ piece and glue it to the left side of the page below the title.

5. Cut out the *numerator* and *denominator* flaps. Apply glue to the back of the top sections and attach them to the page so that the arrows point to the correct parts of the fraction piece.

6. Under the flaps, write short definitions for *numerator* and *denominator*.

7. Cut out the square with one-fourth shaded. Glue it to the right of the labeled $\frac{1}{4}$ piece.

8. Discuss the parts of a fraction and how they relate to the shaded fraction.

9. Cut out the *Fractions describe* flap book. Apply glue to the back of the center section and attach it to the middle of the page. Cut out the two blank pieces. Glue one under each flap.

10. Discuss why it is important for a fraction to be divided equally. Under the flaps, divide the blank pieces to show an example and a non-example of a fraction.

11. Cut out the *Write each fraction* flap book. Cut on the solid lines to create five flaps. Apply glue to the back of the top section and attach it to the bottom of the page.

12. Under each flap, write the fraction.

Reflect on Learning

To complete the left-hand page, have students copy the partitioned rectangles from the introduction into their notebooks. Then, students should color one section of each rectangle and write the fraction for each.

Understanding Fractions

Fractions are _____ that describe _____ of a _____ .

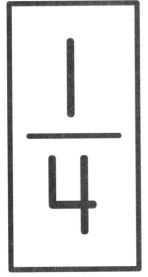

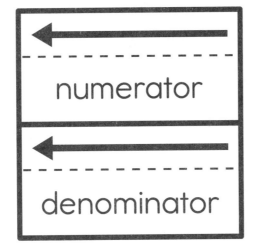

numerator

denominator

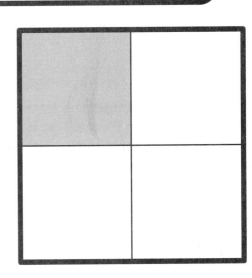

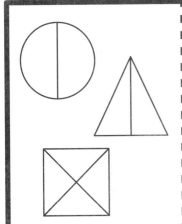

Fractions describe **equal** parts of a whole.

These are fractions.

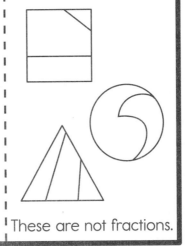

These are not fractions.

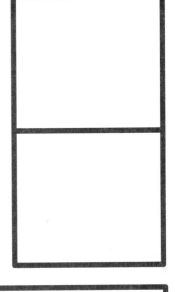

Write each fraction.

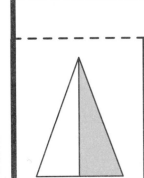

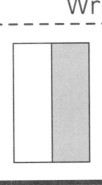

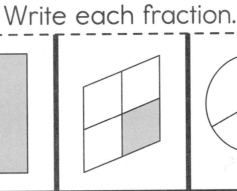

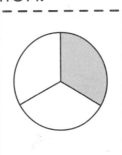

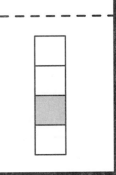

Building Fractions

Introduction

Review the parts of a fraction. Alternate saying *numerator* and *denominator*. Each time students hear *numerator*, they should hold their hands in the air to represent the top part of a fraction. Each time they hear *denominator*, they should hold their hands low to represent the bottom part of a fraction. Then, discuss what each part of a fraction represents.

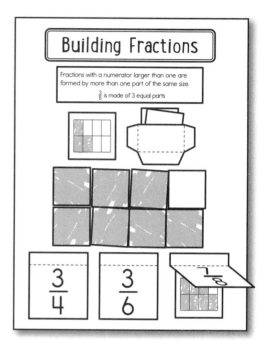

Creating the Notebook Page

Guide students through the following steps to complete the right-hand page in their notebooks.

1. Add a Table of Contents entry for the Building Fractions pages.

2. Cut out the title and glue it to the top of the page.

3. Cut out the *Fractions with* piece and glue it below the title.

4. Cut out the piece with the rectangle divided into eighths and glue it to the left side of the page below the *Fractions with* piece.

5. Discuss how fractions with a numerator greater than 1 are formed by more than one equal-sized part. Shade the fraction piece to show $\frac{3}{8}$.

6. Color the large rectangle with eight sections before cutting it out. Cut out the large rectangle. Cut on the solid lines to create eight colored square pieces.

7. Cut out the pocket. Apply glue to the back of the tabs and attach it to the right side of the page below the *Fractions with* piece.

8. Place the squares facedown in a rectangle on the page. Flip them faceup to show fractions such as $\frac{2}{8}, \frac{4}{8}, \frac{5}{8}$, etc. Remove some squares to work with fourths and sixths as well. Store the squares in the pocket when not in use.

9. Cut out the flaps. Apply glue to the back of the top sections and attach them to the bottom of the page. Cut out the fraction squares and glue each one under the corresponding flap.

10. Use the colored squares to represent the fraction on each flap. Then, color the fraction under each flap to match.

Reflect on Learning

To complete the left-hand page, have students write how many equal parts form each of the fractions on the flaps on the right-hand page. For example, $\frac{3}{8}$ *is made of 3 equal parts*.

Building Fractions

Fractions with a numerator larger than one are formed by more than one part of the same size.

$\frac{3}{8}$ is made of 3 equal parts

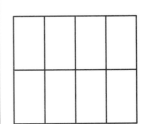

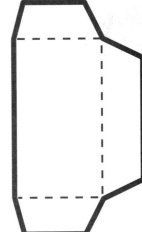

$\frac{3}{4}$

$\frac{3}{6}$

$\frac{7}{8}$

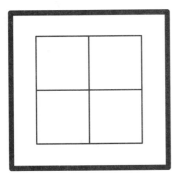

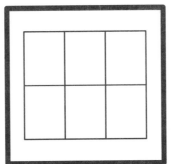

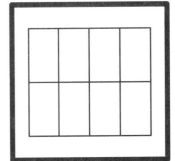

Fractions on a Number Line

Introduction

Provide each student with a small piece of paper such as an index card or a self-stick note. Ask students to identify how many pieces of paper they each have (1). Then, have students use a pencil to partition the paper into two equal shares. Have each student carefully tear the paper along the pencil line to divide the paper into halves. Discuss the fraction of the original paper that each piece represents ($\frac{1}{2}$). Is it more than 0? More than 1? Less than 1?

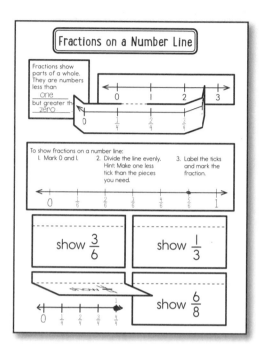

Creating the Notebook Page

Guide students through the following steps to complete the right-hand page in their notebooks.

1. Add a Table of Contents entry for the Fractions on a Number Line pages.

2. Cut out the title and glue it to the top of the page.

3. Cut out the *Fractions show* piece and glue it to the left side of the page below the title.

4. Cut out the double number line piece. Cut on the solid lines to create a flap. Fold the bottom number line on each tick mark so that it folds up and fits between the 0 and 1 space. Apply glue to the back of the top number line and attach it to the right of the *Fractions show* piece.

5. Discuss how fractions almost always represent numbers between 0 and 1. Complete the explanation. (They are numbers less than **one** but greater than **zero**.) Look at the number line piece. Unfold the bottom number line to show how a fraction number line "hides" between 0 and 1. Label the tick marks on the fraction number line with fourths.

6. Cut out the *To show fractions on a number line* piece and glue it to the middle of the page.

7. Discuss how to divide a number line. Follow the steps to divide the number line to show a fraction of your choosing such as $\frac{5}{6}$.

8. Cut out the flaps. Apply glue to the back of the top sections and attach them to the bottom of the page.

9. Under each flap, draw a number line and label it to show the fraction on the flap.

Reflect on Learning

To complete the left-hand page, have students draw number lines to show where they would place the fractions $\frac{3}{1}$ and $\frac{4}{4}$. Then, have students write explanations to describe why they chose to place the fractions where they did.

Fractions show parts of a whole. They are numbers less than

_____

but greater than

_____ .

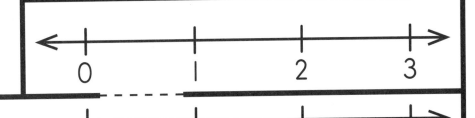

To show fractions on a number line:

1. Mark 0 and 1.

2. Divide the line evenly. Hint: Make one less tick than the pieces you need.

3. Label the ticks and mark the fraction.

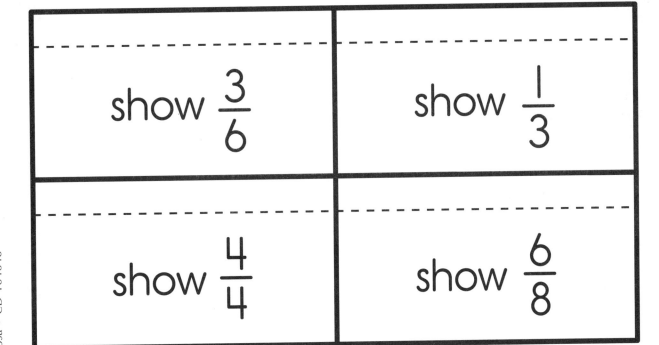

show $\frac{3}{6}$

show $\frac{1}{3}$

show $\frac{4}{4}$

show $\frac{6}{8}$

Representing Fractions

Introduction

Review naming fractions. Draw a rectangle on the board. Divide it into four equal pieces and shade one piece. Have a student name the fraction. Erase the shading and divisions and divide and shade the rectangle to represent a different fraction such as $\frac{3}{6}$. Have a different student name the new fraction. Repeat several times with different divisions and different shading.

Creating the Notebook Page

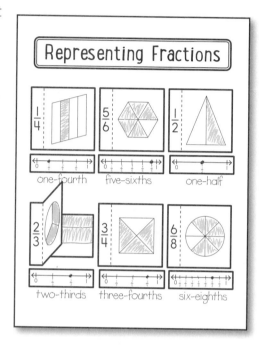

Guide students through the following steps to complete the right-hand page in their notebooks.

1. Add a Table of Contents entry for the Representing Fractions pages.

2. Cut out the title and glue it to the top of the page.

3. Cut out the flaps. Apply glue to the back of the left sections and attach them to the page, leaving space under each one.

4. Cut out the blank squares. Glue one under each flap. Cut out the number lines. Glue one below each flap.

5. Look at the fraction on each flap. Color the shape on each flap to show the fraction. Under the flap, divide the square and shade it to show the fraction. Then, divide the number line and label it to show the fraction. Finally, write the fraction in words below the number line.

Reflect on Learning

To complete the left-hand page, draw two circles on the board and shade one. Explain how it represents one-half, because one of the two pieces is shaded. Have students use parts of a set to draw representations for the remaining five fractions from the right-hand page.

Representing Fractions

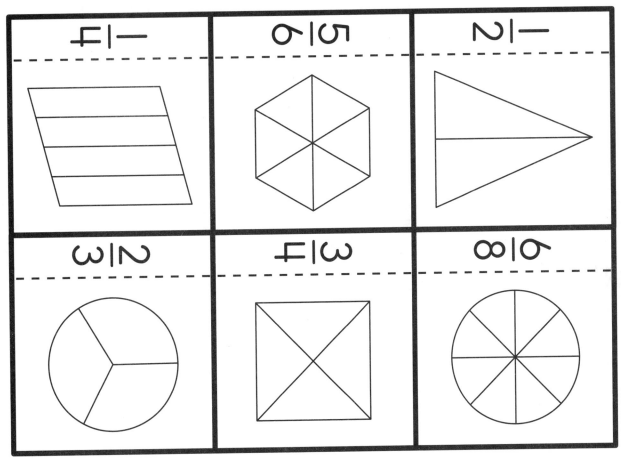

$\frac{1}{4}$ $\frac{5}{6}$ $\frac{1}{2}$

$\frac{2}{3}$ $\frac{3}{4}$ $\frac{6}{8}$

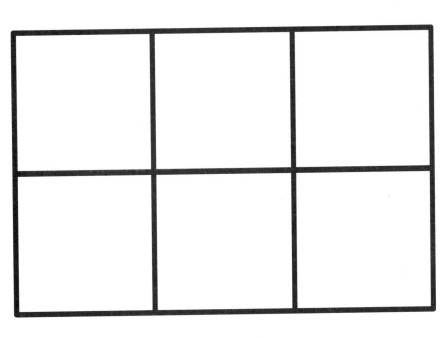

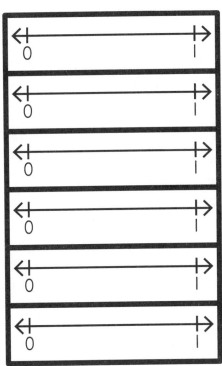

Fractions and Whole Numbers

Display pictures of several pieces of the same type of food with equal parts, such as segmented oranges, chocolate bars, or sliced pizzas. Draw attention to one of the images and discuss how it shows a fraction. For example, the pizza has eight slices. One slice is $\frac{1}{8}$ of the pizza. Then, look at the group of food as a whole. Challenge students to figure out how it would be represented as a fraction. As a class, discuss how fractions can be parts of whole numbers in everyday life.

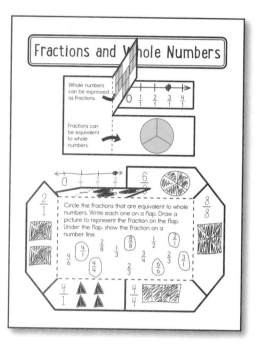

Creating the Notebook Page

Guide students through the following steps to complete the right-hand page in their notebooks.

1. Add a Table of Contents entry for the Fractions and Whole Numbers pages.

2. Cut out the title and glue it to the top of the page.

3. Cut out the *Whole numbers can* flap book. Cut on the solid line to create two flaps. Apply glue to the back of the left section and attach it below the title. Cut out the number lines. Glue the fourths number line under the top flap and glue the thirds number line under the bottom flap.

4. Discuss the two ways whole numbers and fractions are related. Look at the example on each flap and describe how it is related to the number line under the flap. Mark the fraction on each number line.

5. Cut out the flap book. Cut on the solid lines to create six flaps. Apply glue to the back of the center section and attach it to the bottom of the page.

6. Follow the directions to complete the flap book. You may need to draw the number lines on the left and right flaps sideways.

Reflect on Learning

To complete the left-hand page, have students return to the images of the food from the introduction. Students should write the fraction that represents the single piece of food as a fraction equivalent to a whole number (for example, an orange with 8 segments would be written as $\frac{8}{8}$). Then, students should write a fraction to represent the entire group of food (for example, 4 oranges would be written as $\frac{4}{1}$).

Fractions and Whole Numbers

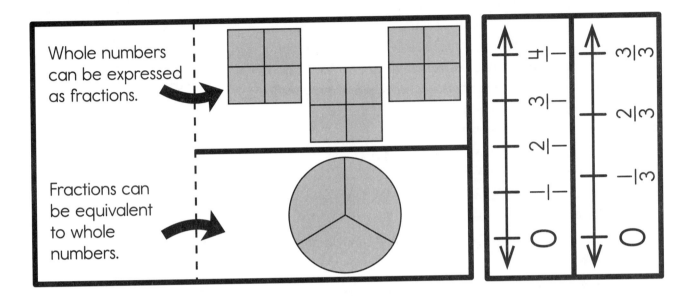

Whole numbers can be expressed as fractions.

Fractions can be equivalent to whole numbers.

Circle the fractions that are equivalent to whole numbers. Write each one on a flap. Draw a picture to represent the fraction on the flap. Under the flap, show the fraction on a number line.

$\frac{4}{1}$ $\frac{2}{8}$ $\frac{1}{3}$ $\frac{8}{8}$ $\frac{1}{2}$ $\frac{2}{1}$

$\frac{4}{6}$ $\frac{4}{4}$ $\frac{2}{3}$ $\frac{3}{4}$ $\frac{2}{3}$ $\frac{3}{1}$ $\frac{6}{6}$

Equivalent Fractions

Introduction

Display a picture of a sandwich divided into four equal parts. Ask students how they would share it with a friend if they had to divide the four parts in half. Discuss what fraction the sandwich is already divided into and how that is different from $\frac{1}{2}$. Ask students how they knew how to fairly divide the sandwich and how they knew each share would still be equal.

Creating the Notebook Page

Guide students through the following steps to complete the right-hand page in their notebooks.

1. Add a Table of Contents entry for the Equivalent Fractions pages.

2. Cut out the title and glue it to the top of the page.

3. Complete the definition of *equivalent fractions* (fractions that are **equal**).

4. Cut out the four flaps. Apply glue to the gray glue sections and stack the flaps with halves on top and eighths on the bottom to create a four-flap book. Glue it to the left side of the page below the title.

5. Cut out the number line piece and glue it to the right of the flap book.

6. Color each fraction in the flap book to show $\frac{1}{2}$, $\frac{2}{4}$, $\frac{3}{6}$, and $\frac{4}{8}$, always coloring the same section of each shape. Label the number lines to show each fraction in the flap book. Discuss what you notice about the fractions. On the page below, write $\frac{1}{2} = \frac{2}{4} = \frac{3}{6} = \frac{4}{8}$.

7. Cut out the *These fractions are* flaps. Apply glue to the back of the top sections and attach them to the middle of the page.

8. Look at the pictures on each flap and discuss how it is important for fractions to be from the same whole to be equivalent. Under each flap, describe why the fractions are or are not equivalent.

9. Cut out the flap books. Cut on the solid lines to create four flaps on each book. Apply glue to the back of each center section and attach the flap books to the bottom of the page.

10. Read each flap book and write the answers under the flaps.

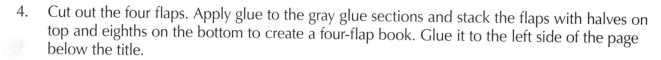

Reflect on Learning

To complete the left-hand page, have students choose a pair of fractions from the *Are these fractions equivalent?* flap book on the right-hand page. Students should draw pictures to support their answers.

Equivalent Fractions

fractions that are _____

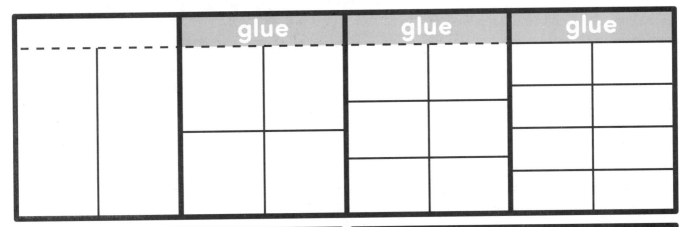
glue   glue   glue

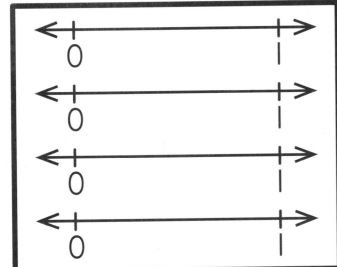

0

0

0

0

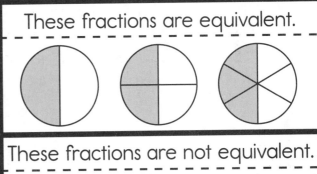

These fractions are equivalent.

These fractions are not equivalent.

$\frac{1}{2}$, $\frac{3}{4}$

$\frac{2}{3}$, $\frac{4}{6}$ Are these fractions equivalent? $\frac{3}{6}$, $\frac{1}{2}$

$\frac{3}{4}$, $\frac{1}{3}$

$\frac{1}{2}$

$\frac{1}{4}$ Write an equivalent fraction. $\frac{1}{3}$

$\frac{2}{3}$

Equivalent Fractions   **47**

Comparing Fractions

Introduction

Review comparing and ordering whole numbers. Provide each student with a self-stick note. Have each student write a three-digit number on the self-stick note. Have pairs of students place their numbers on the board and write <, >, or = between their numbers to compare them. Then, have groups of three or four students place their numbers on the board from least to greatest. Repeat until every student has had a turn.

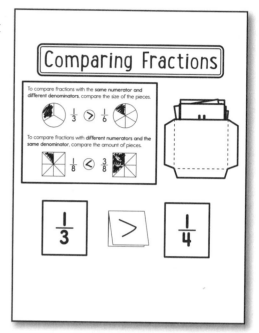

Creating the Notebook Page

Guide students through the following steps to complete the right-hand page in their notebooks.

1. Add a Table of Contents entry for the Comparing Fractions pages.

2. Cut out the title and glue it to the top of the page.

3. Cut out the *To compare fractions* piece. Glue it to the top left of the page.

4. Discuss how to compare fractions in each type of situation. Shade the fractions to match the examples. Then, write <, >, or = to complete the comparisons.

5. Cut out the piece with the equal sign. Fold the bottom and top flaps over the equal sign. Apply glue to the back of the middle section. Attach it to the center of the bottom half of the page so that the flaps open up and down.

6. Flip down the top flap and draw a greater than symbol (>) on it. Flip up the bottom flap and draw a less than symbol (<) on it.

7. Cut out the pocket. Apply glue to the back of the tabs and attach it to the page beside the *To compare fractions* piece.

8. Cut out the fraction cards. Place one card on each side of the symbols piece. Unfold the flaps to create a true number comparison. For more practice, write additional fractions on the backs of the cards. Store the cards in the pocket when not in use.

Reflect on Learning

To complete the left-hand page, have students reflect on why fractions must be from the same whole to be compared to each other.

Comparing Fractions

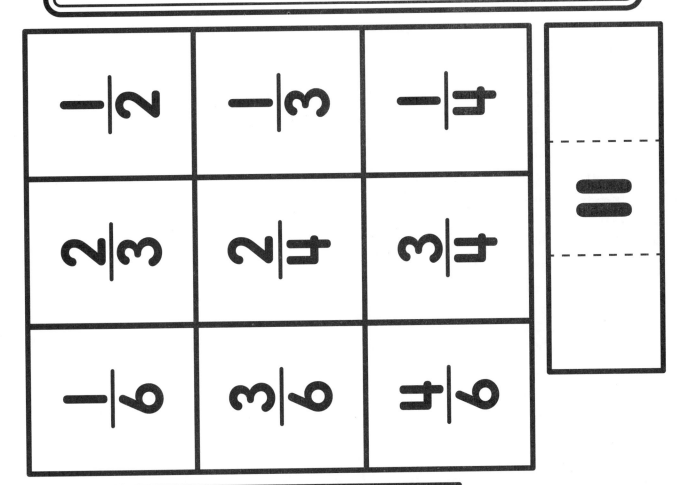

$\frac{1}{2}$	$\frac{1}{3}$	$\frac{1}{4}$
$\frac{2}{3}$	$\frac{2}{4}$	$\frac{3}{4}$
$\frac{1}{6}$	$\frac{3}{6}$	$\frac{4}{6}$

$=$

To compare fractions with the **same numerator and different denominators**, compare the size of the pieces.

 $\frac{1}{3}$ $\frac{1}{6}$

To compare fractions with **different numerators and the same denominator**, compare the amount of pieces.

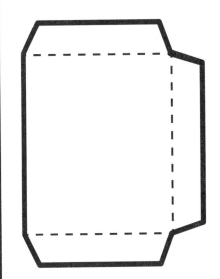

Adding and Subtracting Fractions

Introduction

Divide students into pairs. Provide each pair with a blank sheet of paper and a colored index card or self-stick note. Have each pair cut the paper and the index card into four equal parts each. Then, challenge students to add one piece of the paper to three pieces of the index card to make a whole. As a class, discuss why students could not create a whole from the different pieces.

Adding and Subtracting Fractions

ATTENTION! Before you add or subtract fractions, look at the denominators. Fractions must be from the same whole before they can be added or subtracted.

$$\frac{1}{6} + \frac{4}{6} = \frac{5}{6}$$ Draw it.

Use a number line.

$$\frac{7}{8} - \frac{2}{8} = \frac{5}{8}$$

Use a number line.

Creating the Notebook Page

Guide students through the following steps to complete the right-hand page in their notebooks.

1. Add a Table of Contents entry for the Adding and Subtracting Fractions pages.

2. Cut out the title and glue it to the top of the page.

3. Cut out the *Attention!* piece and glue it below the title.

4. Discuss what it means to be from the same whole and why it is important for fractions to be from the same whole before they are added or subtracted.

5. Cut out the addition and subtraction pieces. Cut on the solid lines to create two flaps on each piece. Apply glue to the back of the top-left sections and attach them to the page.

6. Cut out the number lines and glue them under the *number line* flaps.

7. Look at each problem. Under the *Draw it* flap, draw a picture to represent the problem. Under the *Use a number line* flap, mark the number line to show the problem. Then, write the answer to each problem on the piece.

Reflect on Learning

To complete the left-hand page, have students explain why fractions must be from the same whole to add or subtract them.

Adding and Subtracting Fractions

ATTENTION!

Before you add or subtract fractions, look at the denominators. Fractions must be from the same whole before they can be added or subtracted.

$$\frac{1}{6} + \frac{4}{6} = \frac{\quad}{\quad}$$

Draw it.

Use a number line.

$$\frac{7}{8} - \frac{2}{8} = \frac{\quad}{\quad}$$

Draw it.

Use a number line.

Time

Introduction

Provide students with paper plates. Have students create clock faces on the plates by labeling the numbers. Say different times to the nearest 5 minutes, such as *5:45*, *6:05*, *7:20*, etc. Students should draw hands on the paper plates to show each time, using a different color for each time.

Creating the Notebook Page

Guide students through the following steps to complete the right-hand page in their notebooks.

1. Add a Table of Contents entry for the Time pages.

2. Cut out the title and glue it to the top of the page.

3. Cut out the two flap books. Cut on the solid lines to create four flaps on each flap book. Apply glue to the gray glue section and place the other flap book on top to create a stacked flap book. Apply glue to the back of the center section and attach it to the page below the title.

4. Under each flap, rewrite the time from the flap above on the analog or digital clock. Then, under the bottom flap, write the time in words.

5. Cut out the three clock flaps. Apply glue to the back of the top sections and attach them to the bottom of the page.

6. Read the problem on each clock. Solve the problem under the flap.

Reflect on Learning

To complete the left-hand page, have students figure out how much time they spend on certain subjects and activities each day. On the board, write the starting and ending times for each block of time during the day such as lunch, recess, specials, reading, math, science, etc. Then, students should use the times to figure out how long each subject takes.

Time

glue

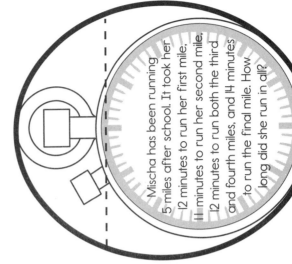

Mischa has been running 5 miles after school. It took her 12 minutes to run her first mile, 11 minutes to run her second mile, 12 minutes to run both the third and fourth miles, and 14 minutes to run the final mile. How long did she run in all?

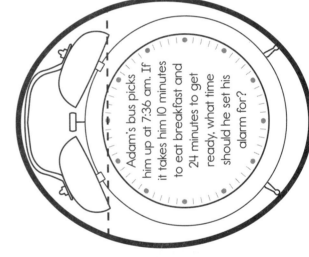

Adam's bus picks him up at 7:36 am. If it takes him 10 minutes to eat breakfast and 24 minutes to get ready, what time should he set his alarm for?

Rose's family is having a yard sale. Rose helped for 10 minutes each hour for 4 hours. Her brother Raul helped for 7 minutes each hour for 6 hours. Who helped longer?

Money

Introduction

Place plastic coins in several paper bags. Divide students into small groups. Give each group a paper bag. Have each student reach into the bag and grab a handful of coins. Students should then add the total value of their handfuls of coins. Have students return their coins to the bag and repeat one more time.

Creating the Notebook Page

Guide students through the following steps to complete the right-hand page in their notebooks.

1. Add a Table of Contents entry for the Money pages.

2. Cut out the title and glue it to the top of the page.

3. Cut out the pocket flaps. Apply glue to the back of the top sections and attach them to the page.

4. Count the money on each flap and write the total on the top of each flap. Then, read the problem on each flap. Solve the problem under the flap.

Reflect on Learning

To complete the left-hand page, have students pretend that they have $5 to spend. Display an ad from a dollar store. Have students list what they would buy, the total amount, and the money they would have left.

© Carson-Dellosa • CD-104648

Money

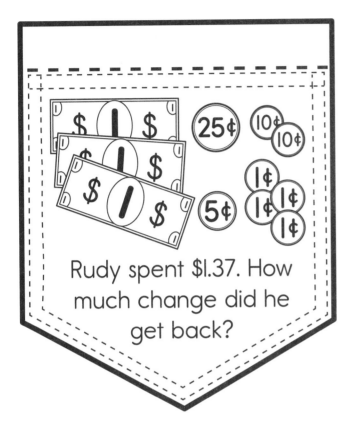

Rudy spent $1.37. How much change did he get back?

Addie spent $2.45. How much money did she have left?

Kami found $2.29. How much money does she have now?

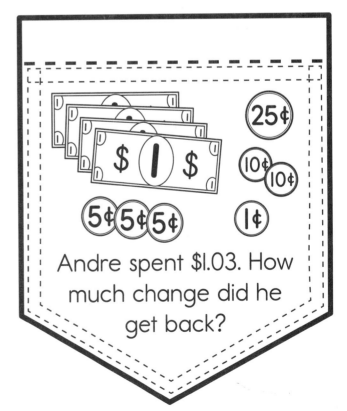

Andre spent $1.03. How much change did he get back?

Picture Graphs and Bar Graphs

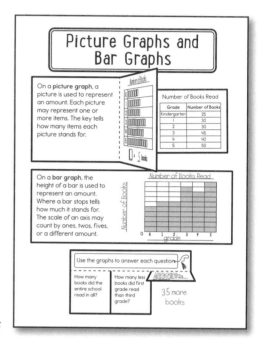
© Carson-Dellosa • CD-104648

Picture Graphs and Bar Graphs

On a **picture graph**, a picture is used to represent an amount. Each picture may represent one or more items. The key tells how many items each picture stands for.

K	
1	
2	
3	
4	
5	

📖 = _____ books

On a **bar graph**, the height of a bar is used to represent an amount. Where a bar stops tells how much it stands for. The scale of an axis may count by ones, twos, fives, or a different amount.

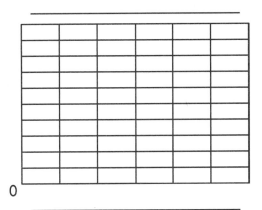

0

Number of Books Read

Grade	Number of Books
Kindergarten	25
1	30
2	30
3	45
4	40
5	50

Use the graphs to answer each question.

How many books did the entire school read in all?

How many less books did first grade read than third grade?

How many more books did third and fourth grade read than fifth grade?

Measuring Mass and Liquid Volume

Introduction

Ask students what unit their height is usually measured in. Repeat for things such as the weight of produce, the amount of milk in a jug, larger bottles of soda, the amount of ice cream in a container, the weight of a bag of chips, etc. If possible, bring in several packages for students to see the measurements on the packaging. Discuss how the unit is different depending on what is being measured.

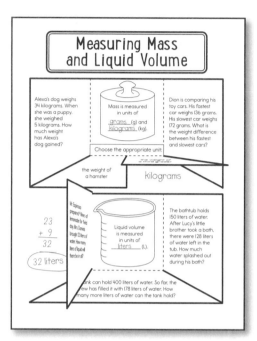

Creating the Notebook Page

Guide students through the following steps to complete the right-hand page in their notebooks.

1. Add a Table of Contents entry for the Measuring Mass and Liquid Volume pages.

2. Cut out the title and glue it to the top of the page.

3. Cut out the *Mass* flap book. Cut on the solid lines to create four flaps. Apply glue to the back of the center section and attach it below the title.

4. Discuss what mass is, what it can measure, and what units it is measured in. Complete the description. [Mass is measured in units of **grams** (g) and **kilograms** (kg).]

5. On the outer flaps, solve the word problems. Write each answer under the flap. On the center flaps, write the appropriate units under the flaps.

6. Cut out the *Liquid volume* flap book. Cut on the solid lines to create three flaps. Apply glue to the back of the center section and attach it below the *Mass* flap book.

7. Discuss what liquid volume is, what it can measure, and what unit it is measured in. Complete the description. [Liquid volume is measured in units of **liters** (L).]

8. Solve the word problem on each flap. Write the answer under each flap.

Reflect on Learning

To complete the left-hand page, have students list three things that would be measured in each of the following: liters, grams, and kilograms.

Answer Key
29 kg; 36 g; hamster, g; third grader, kg
32 L; 222 L; 22 L

Measuring Mass and Liquid Volume

Alexa's dog weighs 34 kilograms. When she was a puppy, she weighed 5 kilograms. How much weight has Alexa's dog gained?

Mass is measured in units of _____ (g) and _____ (kg).

Dion is comparing his toy cars. His fastest car weighs 136 grams. His slowest car weighs 172 grams. What is the weight difference between his fastest and slowest cars?

Choose the appropriate unit:

the weight of a hamster

the weight of a third grader

Mr. Espinoza prepared 9 liters of lemonade for field day. Mrs. Daniels brought 23 liters of water. How many liters of liquid will there be in all?

Liquid volume is measured in units of _____ (L).

The bathtub holds 150 liters of water. After Lucy's little brother took a bath, there were 128 liters of water left in the tub. How much water splashed out during his bath?

A tank can hold 400 liters of water. So far, the crew has filled it with 178 liters of water. How many more liters of water can the tank hold?

Measuring and Plotting Length

Introduction

Review how to measure objects. Provide students with rulers. Have each student measure a book in her desk. Emphasize aligning the end of the ruler with one edge of the book. Then, walk students though looking at the mark on the ruler where the object ends and figuring out the measurement. Have students practice measuring several different lengths.

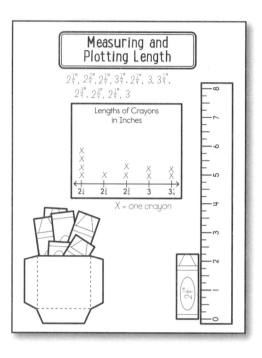

Creating the Notebook Page

Guide students through the following steps to complete the right-hand page in their notebooks.

1. Add a Table of Contents entry for the Measuring and Plotting Length pages.

2. Cut out the title and glue it to the top of the page.

3. Cut out the ruler and glue it along the right side of the page with the tick marks facing in.

4. Cut out the pocket. Apply glue to the back of the tabs and attach it to the bottom-left corner of the page.

5. Cut out the crayons. Use the ruler to measure each crayon. Write the measurement of each crayon on the crayon and on the page below the title. Store the crayons in the pocket created in step 4.

6. Cut out the line plot and attach it to the middle of the page.

7. Discuss how to create a line plot. Below the line plot, write *X = one crayon*. Using the data above, plot an X for each crayon on the line plot.

Reflect on Learning

To complete the left-hand page, have each student draw a Venn diagram. Students should label one side *Line Plots* and the other side *Bar Graphs*. Students should complete the Venn diagrams by comparing and contrasting line plots and bar graphs. Then, each student should write a sentence to explain why a line plot is useful for showing lengths of objects.

Measuring and Plotting Length

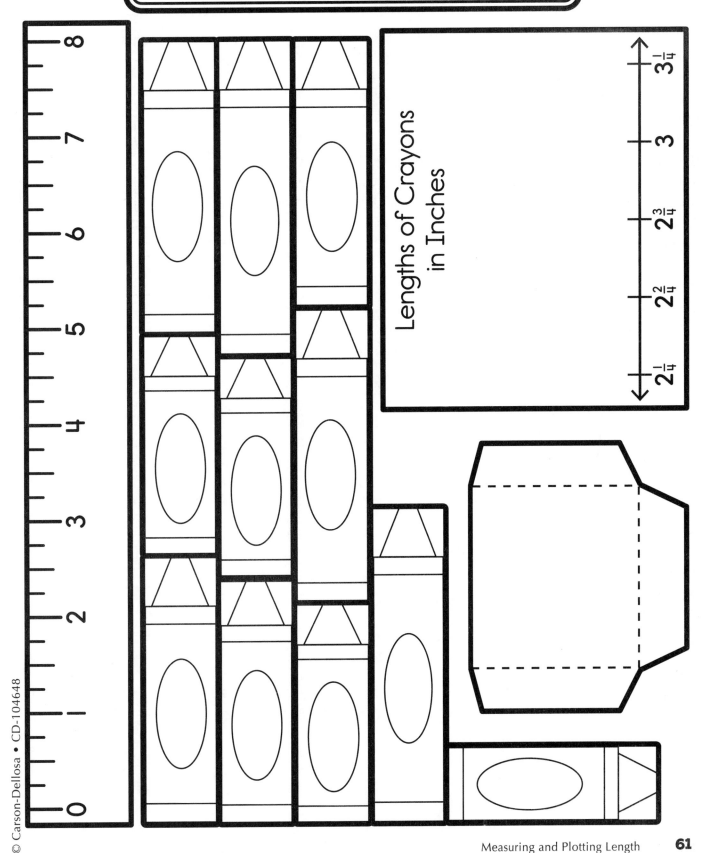

Lengths of Crayons in Inches

Understanding Area

Introduction

Draw a small rectangle on the board. Tell students they are going to cover that section of the board with square self-stick notes. Provide a student with a ruler to measure the space before providing the self-stick notes he will need. Have the student tell you his measurement and give him the amount of self-stick notes that match the measurement. Most likely, he will give you a length and/or a width. Provide him with the self-stick notes to match the given measurement(s). For example, give 10 self-stick notes for a measurement of 10 inches. As a class, discuss why the measurement wouldn't cover the section. Explain that area is the measurement that measures the space covered by something.

Creating the Notebook Page

Guide students through the following steps to complete the right-hand page in their notebooks.

1. Add a Table of Contents entry for the Understanding Area pages.

2. Cut out the title and glue it to the top of the page.

3. Cut out the *Area is* flap book. Cut on the solid lines to create four flaps. Apply glue to the back of the top section and attach it below the title.

4. Discuss what area is. Complete the sentences. (Area is the **space** a shape takes up. It is measured in **square units** such as *square inches* or *square centimeters.*) Discuss how area should and should not be measured. Under each flap, write if the area is being measured correctly, and why or why not.

5. Cut out the flaps. Apply glue to the back of the top sections and attach them to the bottom of the page.

6. Find the area of the shape on each flap. Write the area under the flap.

Reflect on Learning

To complete the left-hand page, have students list several real-world scenarios where it would be useful to measure the area of something (for example, carpeting a room or measuring the size of a blanket).

62

Understanding Area

Area is the _____ a shape takes up. It is measured in _____
_____ such as *square inches* or *square centimeters*.

To measure area, count the number of squares it takes to cover the shape.
The squares must touch along the edges with no overlap and no gaps.

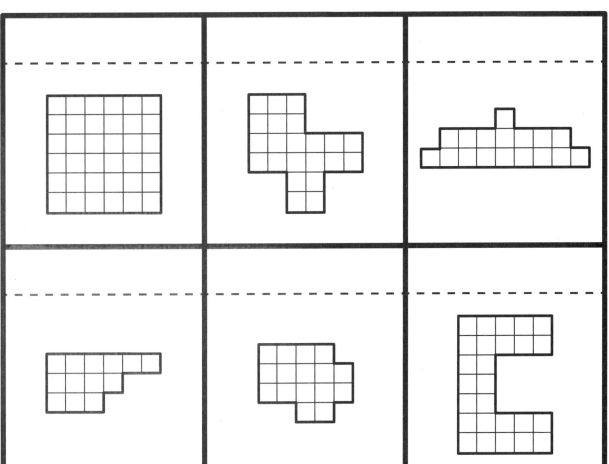

The Formula for Finding Area

Introduction

Provide students with tile manipulatives or have students cut out 10 squares from construction paper or index cards. Draw a 2 by 3 rectangle on the board and have students model it with their tiles on top of a sheet of paper. Discuss what the area of the rectangle is. Then, have students trace around the edge of the shape and trace the tiles. Draw their attention to how there is one less line than there are tiles in each direction. Repeat with a 3 by 3 rectangle.

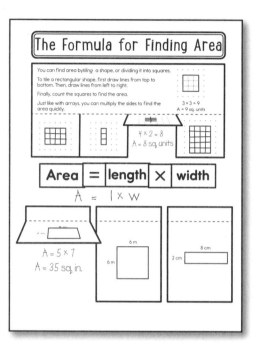

Creating the Notebook Page

Guide students through the following steps to complete the right-hand page in their notebooks.

1.   Add a Table of Contents entry for the The Formula for Finding Area pages.

2.   Cut out the title and glue it to the top of the page.

3.   Cut out the *You can find area* flap book. Cut on the solid lines to create four flaps. Apply glue to the back of the top section and attach it below the title.

4.   Discuss how to tile a shape. Look at the example and discuss the relationship between the tiling, arrays, and multiplication sentences. On the flaps, draw lines to tile each shape. Under each flap, write a related multiplication sentence to show the array and find the area.

5.   Cut out the five labels. Glue them in order to show the formula for finding area (Area = length × width). Under the labels, write the abbreviated version of the formula (*A = l × w*).

6.   Cut out the flaps. Apply glue to the back of the top sections and attach them to the bottom of the page.

7.   Under each flap, write the formula to find the area for the rectangle on the flap. Solve.

Reflect on Learning

To complete the left-hand page, have students reflect on how the formula for area is related to multiplication and arrays.

The Formula for Finding Area

You can find area by *tiling* a shape, or dividing it into squares.

To tile a rectangular shape, first draw lines from top to bottom. Then, draw lines from left to right.

Finally, count the squares to find the area.

Just like with arrays, you can multiply the sides to find the area quickly.

$3 \times 3 = 9$

A = 9 sq. units

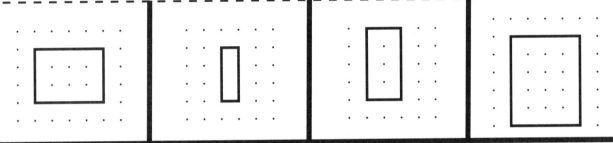

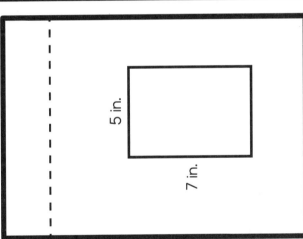

5 in.

7 in.

Area = length × width

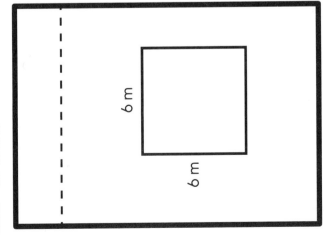

6 m

6 m

8 cm

2 cm

Area of Complex Figures

Introduction

Draw a rectilinear figure on the board. As a class, discuss what shapes it is composed of. Have a student approach the board and draw a line or lines to separate the figure into two or more simpler shapes. Erase the line(s) and have another student draw different lines to separate the shape into two or more different shapes. Draw a different rectilinear figure on the board and repeat.

Creating the Notebook Page

Guide students through the following steps to complete the right-hand page in their notebooks.

1. Add a Table of Contents entry for the Area of Complex Figures pages.

2. Cut out the title and glue it to the top of the page.

3. Cut out the *Area is additive* piece and glue it to the top-left side of the page below the title.

4. Complete the explanation. (This means areas of figures can be **added** together.)

5. Cut out the two rectangular flaps. Apply glue to the gray glue section and place the other flap directly on top to create a two-flap book. Apply glue to the back of the left section and attach it to the page beside the explanation piece.

6. Discuss how the figure on the top flap can be split into two rectangles. Lift the flap and look at the split figure. Return to the first flap and draw a line to show where the complex figure was split. Lift the flap and find the areas of the two rectangles. Show your work under the flap. Add the areas to get the total area of the original figure.

7. Cut out the two-flap piece. Cut on the solid line to create two flaps. Apply glue to the back of the left section and attach it to the bottom of the page.

8. Discuss how shapes can be split in more than one way. Use two different colors to draw lines on the original figure to show how it was split on each flap. Under each flap, find the total area. Discuss if splitting the shape in different ways affected the final area.

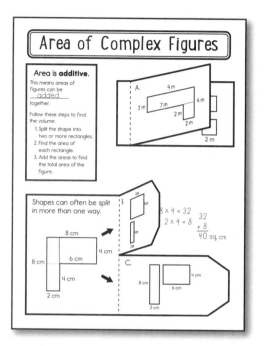

Reflect on Learning

To complete the left-hand page, draw a U-shaped rectilinear figure and a rectangle with a rectangular hole in the middle on the board. Have students explain how they would find the area of each shape.

Answer Key
A. 22 sq. m; B. 32 sq. cm, 8 sq. cm; 40 sq. cm; C. 16 sq. cm, 24 sq. cm; 40 sq. cm

Area of Complex Figures

Area is **additive**.

This means areas of figures can be

_____

together.

Follow these steps to find the volume:

1. Split the shape into two or more rectangles.
2. Find the area of each rectangle.
3. Add the areas to find the total area of the figure.

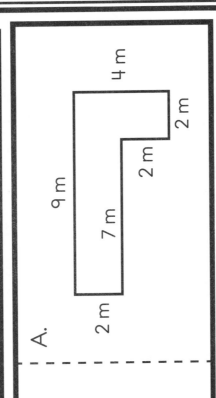

A.

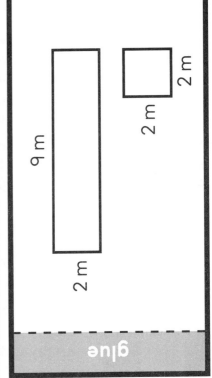

glue

Shapes can often be split in more than one way.

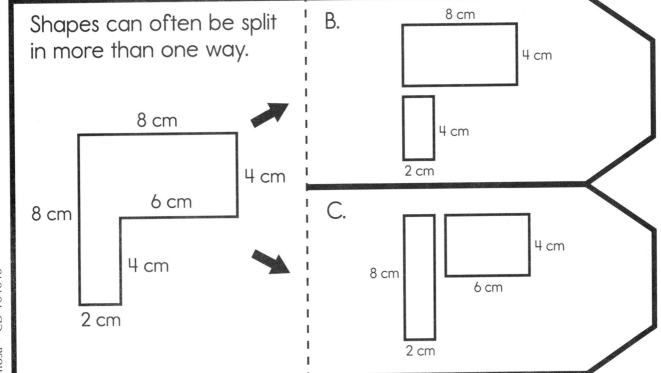

B.

C.

Understanding Perimeter

Introduction

Tell students to pretend that they get to place decorative borders around the edge of their desks. Display a strip of border as a sample. Provide students with rulers and challenge them to figure out what they would need to measure to find the total amount of border they would need to order for their desks. As a class, discuss what students chose to measure, why, and what totals they found.

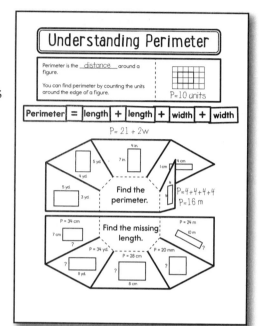

Creating the Notebook Page

Guide students through the following steps to complete the right-hand page in their notebooks.

1.   Add a Table of Contents entry for the Understanding Perimeter pages.

2.   Cut out the title and glue it to the top of the page.

3.   Cut out the *Perimeter is* flap. Apply glue to the back of the left section and attach it to the page below the title.

4.   Discuss what perimeter is and complete the definition. (Perimeter is the **distance** around a figure.) Discuss how to find the perimeter of a rectangle. Look at the example to the right and find the perimeter by counting. Write it on the flap below the art.

5.   Cut out the nine labels. Glue them in order to show the formula for finding perimeter (Perimeter = length + length + width + width). Below the labels, write an abbreviated version of the formula (***P = l + l + w + w*** or ***P = 2l + 2w***). Use the formula to find the perimeter of the rectangle on the flap of the *Perimeter is* piece. Write the formula and answer under the flap. Discuss how the perimeter found is the same as when the units were counted in step 4.

6.   Cut out the flap books. Cut on the lines to create five flaps on each flap book. Apply glue to the back of the center sections and attach them to the bottom of the page.

7.   Follow the directions on each flap book. Write the answers under the flaps.

Reflect on Learning

To complete the left-hand page, have students list several real-world scenarios where it would be useful to measure the perimeter of something (for example, fencing in a yard or finding the distance someone walked around a field).

Answer Key
Find the perimeter (from left to right): 16 yd.; 18 yd.; 22 in.; 10 cm; 16 m
Find the missing length (from left to right): 10 cm; 6 yd.; 6 cm; 5 mm; 2 m

Understanding Perimeter

Perimeter is the _____ around a figure.

You can find perimeter by counting the units around the edge of a figure.

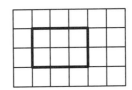

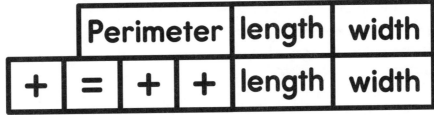

				length	width
Perimeter				length	width
+	=	+	+	length	width

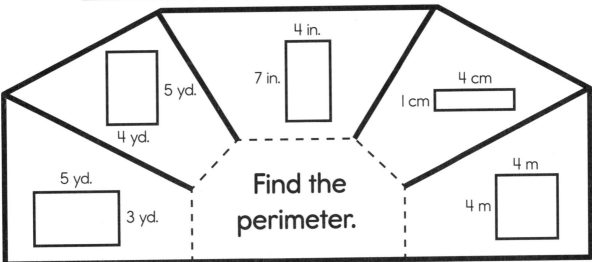

Find the perimeter.

5 yd.
4 yd.

4 in.
7 in.

4 cm
1 cm

4 m
4 m

5 yd.
3 yd.

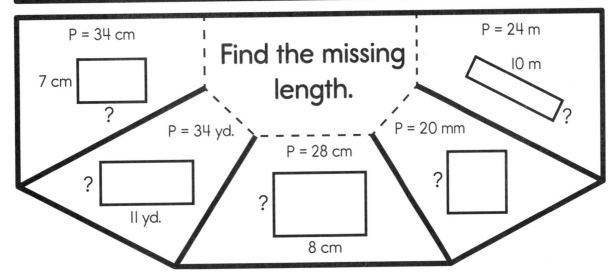

Find the missing length.

P = 34 cm
7 cm
?

P = 24 m
10 m
?

P = 34 yd.
?
11 yd.

P = 28 cm
?
8 cm

P = 20 mm
?

Relating Perimeter and Area

Introduction

Provide each student with an 18-inch length of yarn and an index card. Students should color the index cards to show the area. Then, have students glue the yarn around the edge of the index cards to show the perimeter. They should cut off the excess and set it aside. On the back of the index cards, have students create a key. They should color a patch the same color used for the area and label it *area*. They should glue down the extra yarn and label it *perimeter*. Have students keep the index cards as reference tools.

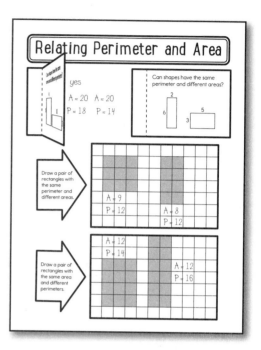

Creating the Notebook Page

Guide students through the following steps to complete the right-hand page in their notebooks.

1. Add a Table of Contents entry for the Relating Perimeter and Area pages.

2. Cut out the title and glue it to the top of the page.

3. Cut out the rectangular flaps. Apply glue to the back of the left sections and attach them below the title.

4. Read the questions on the flaps. Look at the examples on each flap and answer the questions by using the example shapes to solve for area and perimeter under the flap.

5. Cut out the arrows. Glue them to the left side of the page. Cut out the graph paper pieces and glue them to the right side of the page.

6. Complete the challenge on each arrow by drawing a pair of rectangles on the graph paper that satisfy the guidelines. Write the area and perimeter by each rectangle.

Reflect on Learning

To complete the left-hand page, have students reflect on why it is possible for some shapes to have the same perimeter and different areas, and vice versa.

Relating Perimeter and Area

Can shapes have the same area and different perimeters?

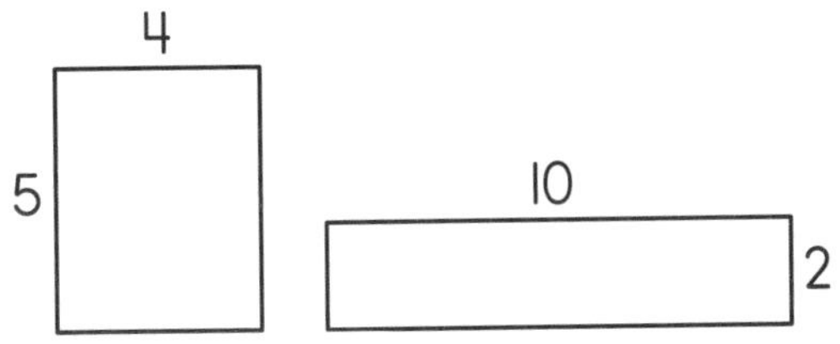

4

5

10

2

Can shapes have the same perimeter and different areas?

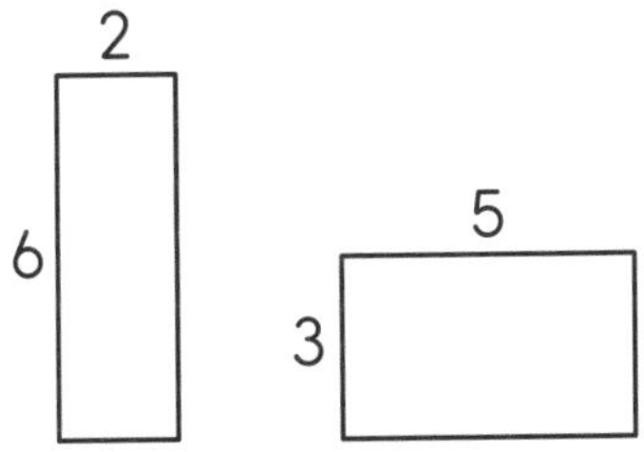

2

6

5

3

Draw a pair of rectangles with the same area and different perimeters.

Draw a pair of rectangles with the same perimeter and different areas.

Attributes of Polygons

Introduction

Provide students with attribute blocks. Have students sort the blocks and describe to partners how they were sorted. Then, have students sort the blocks a different way and describe how they were sorted to different partners. As a class, discuss how shapes have different characteristics, or attributes, that allow us to group them and gather information about them.

Creating the Notebook Page

Guide students through the following steps to complete the right-hand page in their notebooks.

1. Add a Table of Contents entry for the Attributes of Polygons pages.

2. Cut out the title and glue it to the top of the page.

3. Cut out the polygon flaps. Apply glue to the back of each rectangular flap and attach each shape to the page.

4. Trace the dashed line on each shape to close the polygon and show all of the sides. Write the name of the polygon on each shape. Under the flap, write the number of sides and number of vertices.

5. Cut out the flap book. Cut on the solid lines to create three flaps. Apply glue to the back of the top section and attach it to the bottom of the page.

6. Under the two left flaps, write the names of shapes that fit in each category. On the blank flap, write a description of your own category. Write the names of shapes that have the attribute(s) listed under the flap.

Reflect on Learning

To complete the left-hand page, have students find the shapes that fit under both the *four sides and four angles* and the *has right angles* flaps on the right-hand page. Students should describe what is special about these shapes and how they are related to one another.

Attributes of Polygons

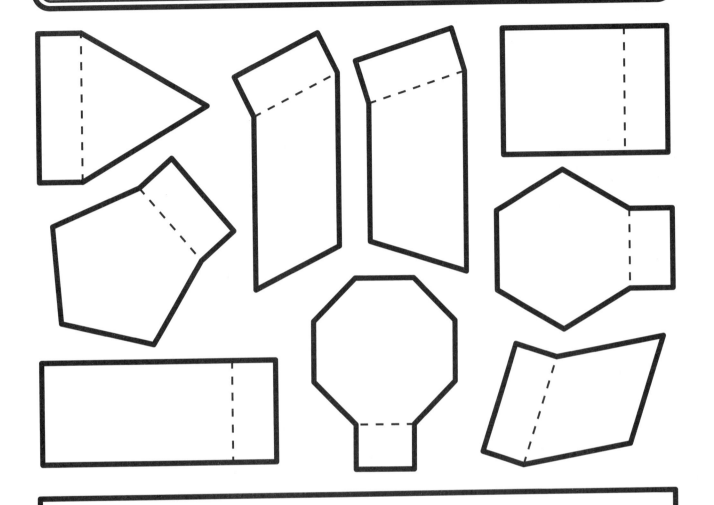

four sides and four angles	has right angles	

Quadrilaterals

Introduction

Before the lesson, create the parts of a polygon attribute chart. Include the number of sides, number of angles, polygon name, and an example picture. Write the information for each place in the chart on an index card. For a square, you would write *4, 4, square* and draw a picture of a square on four separate index cards. Draw the chart headings on the board and give an index card to each student. Have students place their index cards in the correct spots on the chart. Some index cards may fit in more than one space.

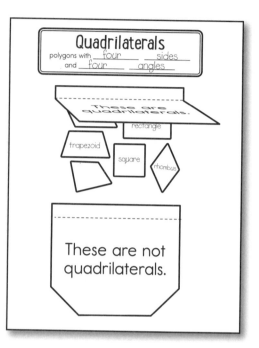

Creating the Notebook Page

Guide students through the following steps to complete the right-hand page in their notebooks.

1. Add a Table of Contents entry for the Quadrilaterals pages.

2. Cut out the title and glue it to the top of the page.

3. Complete the definition of *quadrilaterals* (polygons with **four sides** and **four angles**).

4. Cut out the flaps. Apply glue to the back of the top sections and attach them to the page.

5. Cut out the shape pieces. Write the name of each shape on the piece. Some shapes may not have names.

6. Discuss what makes a shape a quadrilateral. Look at the shapes of the flaps and describe why one is a quadrilateral and the other is not. Sort the shape pieces and glue them under the correct flap. If space allows, draw additional examples under the flaps.

Reflect on Learning

To complete the left-hand page, have students draw several examples of quadrilaterals that are not squares, rectangles, or rhombuses.

Quadrilaterals

polygons with _____ _____

and _____ _____

These are quadrilaterals.

These are not quadrilaterals.

Partitioning Shapes

Introduction

Before the lesson, cut enough 12-inch lengths of yarn for each student to have three. Provide each student with an index card or sheet of paper. Allow students to decorate the paper like a cake. Give each student three pieces of yarn. Challenge students to lay the yarn across their cakes to "cut" them into two equal pieces to share. Discuss the ways different students chose to cut their cakes. Repeat with three and four equal shares.

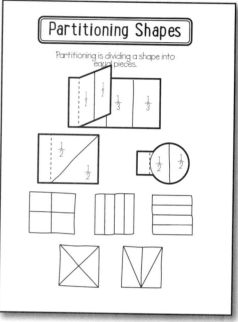

Creating the Notebook Page

Guide students through the following steps to complete the right-hand page in their notebooks.

1. Add a Table of Contents entry for the Partitioning Shapes pages.

2. Cut out the title and glue it to the top of the page.

3. Discuss what partitioning is (dividing a shape into equal pieces). Below the title, write a short definition of partitioning.

4. Cut out the rectangle flaps. Apply glue to the gray glue sections and stack the flaps to create a four-flap book. Apply glue to the back of the left section and attach the flap book below the definition.

5. Partition the top shape in the flap book in half. Then, partition the next pages into thirds, fourths, and sixths. If desired, trace the bottom flap onto the page and partition it into eighths. Color each flap a different color and label each section with the unit fraction.

6. Repeat steps 4 and 5 with the square and circle flaps. Attach them side by side below the rectangle flap book.

7. On the bottom of the page, draw several squares. In each square, draw a different way to partition a square into four equal shares. Draw more squares as needed.

Reflect on Learning

To complete the left-hand page, have students describe how partitioning and fractions are related. Students should explain why it is important for the pieces to always be equal in size and shape.

Partitioning Shapes

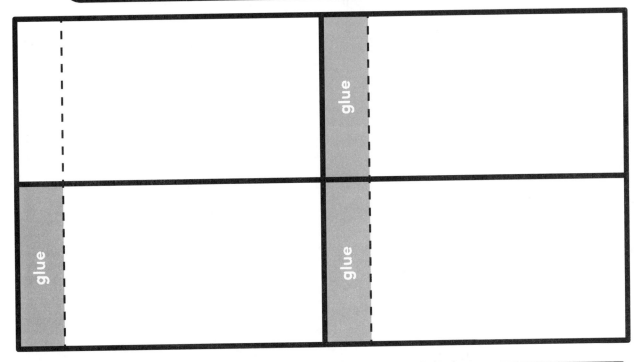

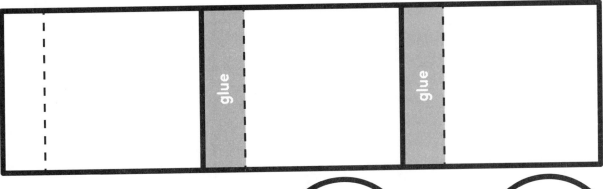

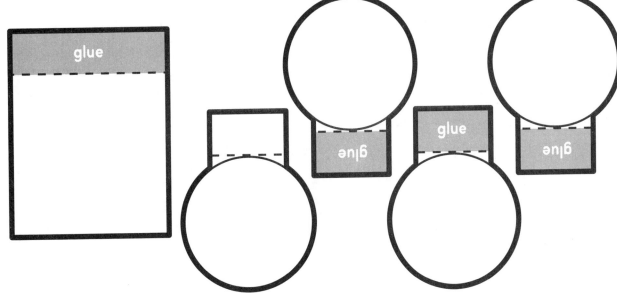

Tabs

Cut out each tab and label it. Apply glue to the back of each tab and align it on the outside edge of the page with only the label section showing beyond the edge. Then, fold each tab to seal the page inside.

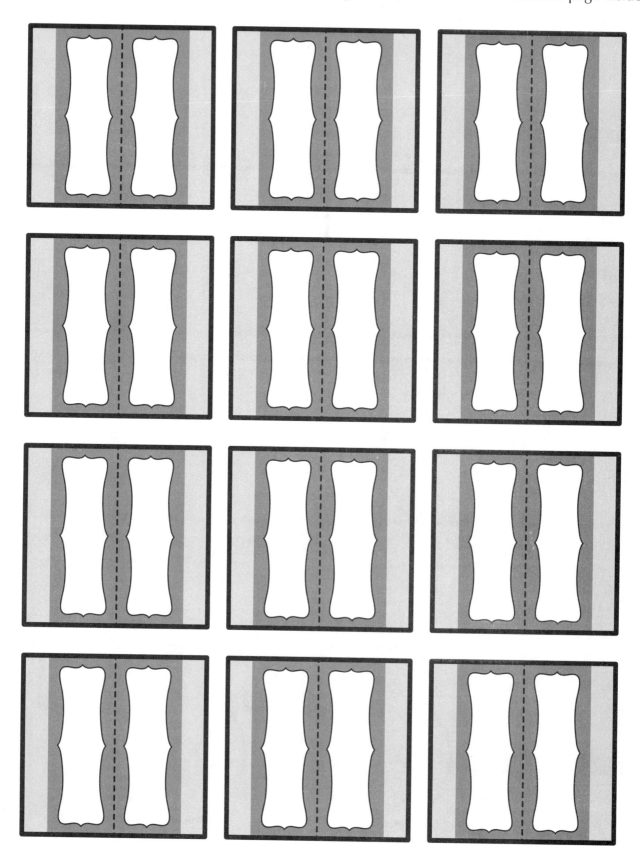

Cut out the KWL chart and cut on the solid lines to create three separate flaps. Apply glue to the back of the Topic section to attach the chart to a notebook page.

What I

Know

What I

Wonder

What I

Learned

Topic:

Library Pocket

Cut out the library pocket on the solid lines. Fold in the side tabs and apply glue to them before folding up the front of the pocket. Apply glue to the back of the pocket to attach it to a notebook page.

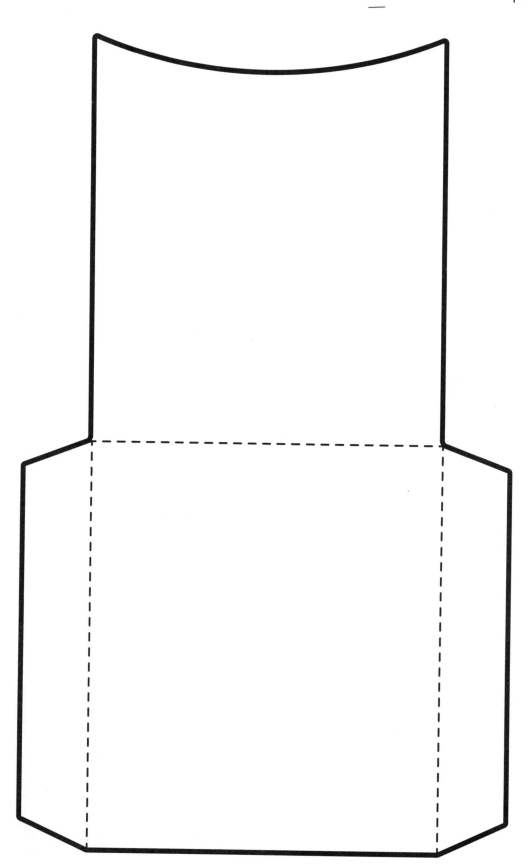

Envelope

Cut out the envelope on the solid lines. Fold in the side tabs and apply glue to them before folding up the rectangular front of the envelope. Fold down the triangular flap to close the envelope. Apply glue to the back of the envelope to attach it to a notebook page.

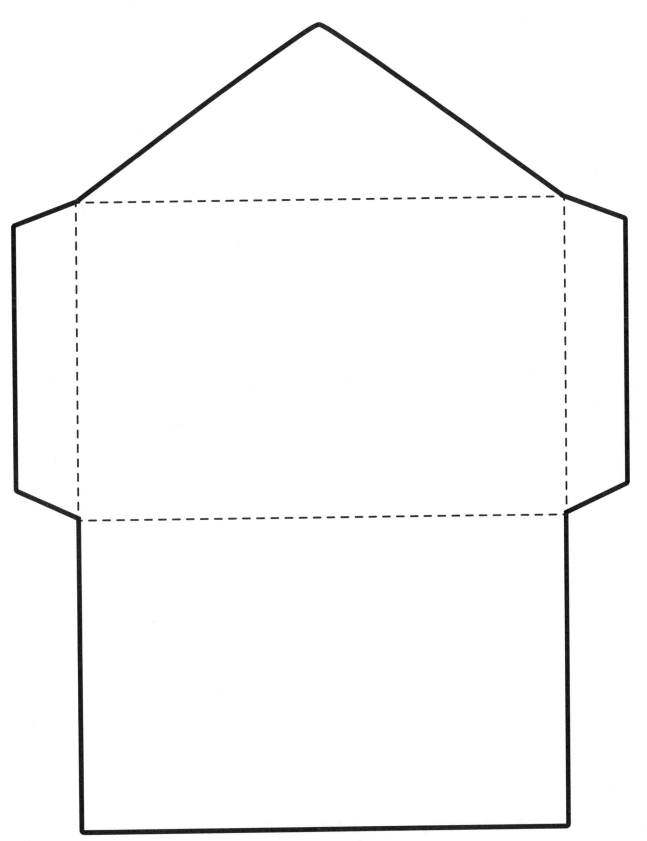

Pocket and Cards

Cut out the pocket on the solid lines. Fold over the front of the pocket. Then, apply glue to the tabs and fold them around the back of the pocket. Apply glue to the back of the pocket to attach it to a notebook page. Cut out the cards and store them in the envelope.

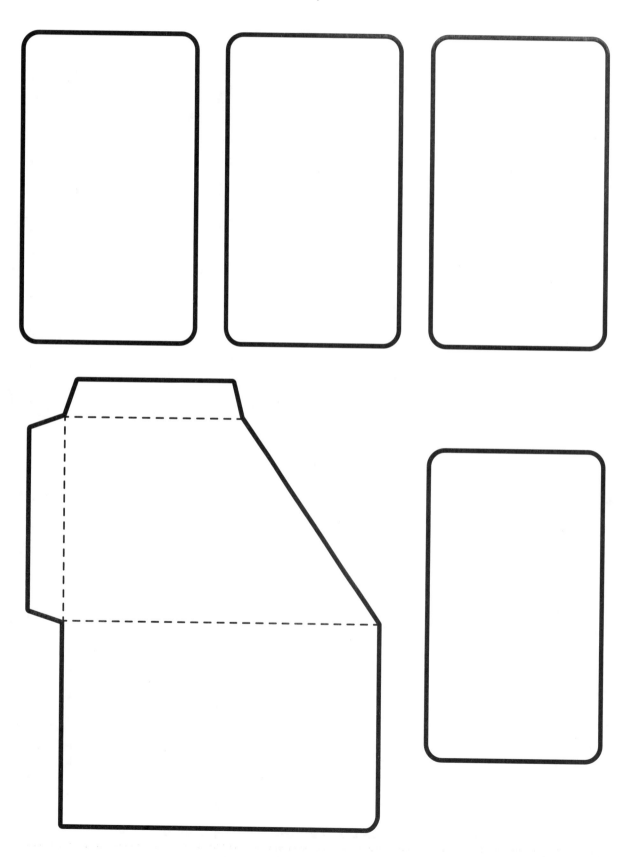

Six-Flap Shutter Fold

Cut out the shutter fold around the outside border. Then, cut on the solid lines to create six flaps. Fold the flaps toward the center. Apply glue to the back of the shutter fold to attach it to a notebook page.

If desired, this template can be modified to create a four-flap shutter fold by cutting off the bottom row. You can also create two three-flap books by cutting it in half down the center line.

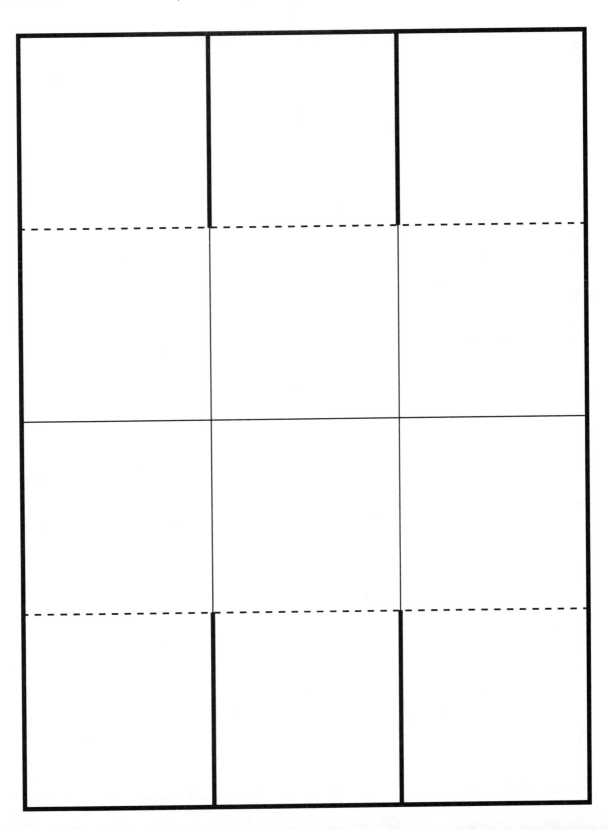

Eight-Flap Shutter Fold

Cut out the shutter fold around the outside border. Then, cut on the solid lines to create eight flaps. Fold the flaps toward the center. Apply glue to the back of the shutter fold to attach it to a notebook page.

If desired, this template can be modified to create two four-flap shutter folds by cutting off the bottom two rows. You can also create two four-flap books by cutting it in half down the center line.

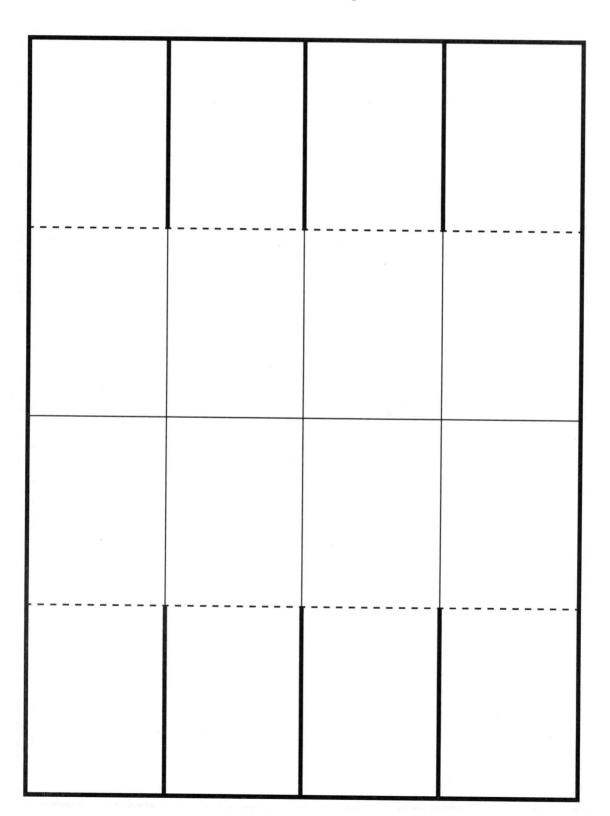

Flap Book—Eight Flaps

Cut out the flap book around the outside border. Then, cut on the solid lines to create eight flaps. Apply glue to the back of the center section to attach it to a notebook page.

If desired, this template can be modified to create a six-flap or two four-flap books by cutting off the bottom row or two. You can also create a tall four-flap book by cutting off the flaps on the left side.

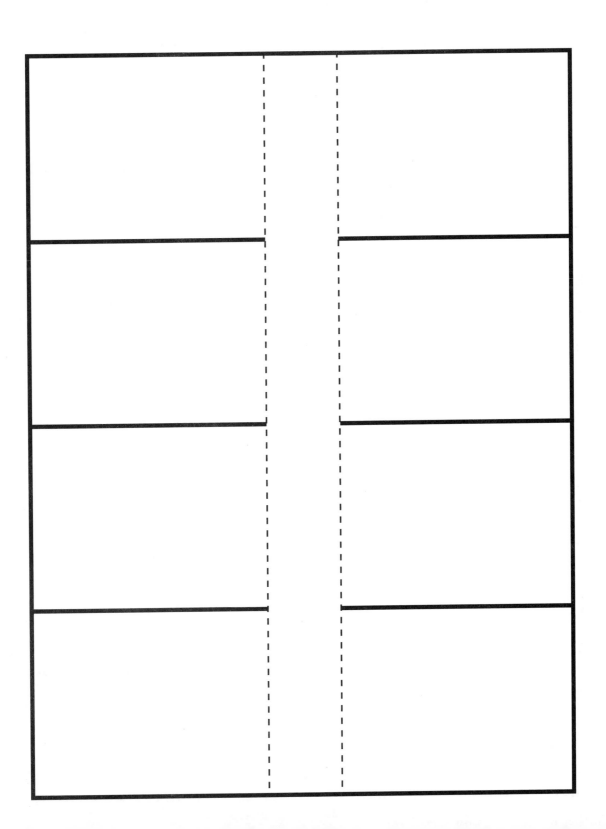

Flap Book—Twelve Flaps

Cut out the flap book around the outside border. Then, cut on the solid lines to create 12 flaps. Apply glue to the back of the center section to attach it to a notebook page.

If desired, this template can be modified to create smaller flap books by cutting off any number of rows from the bottom. You can also create a tall flap book by cutting off the flaps on the left side.

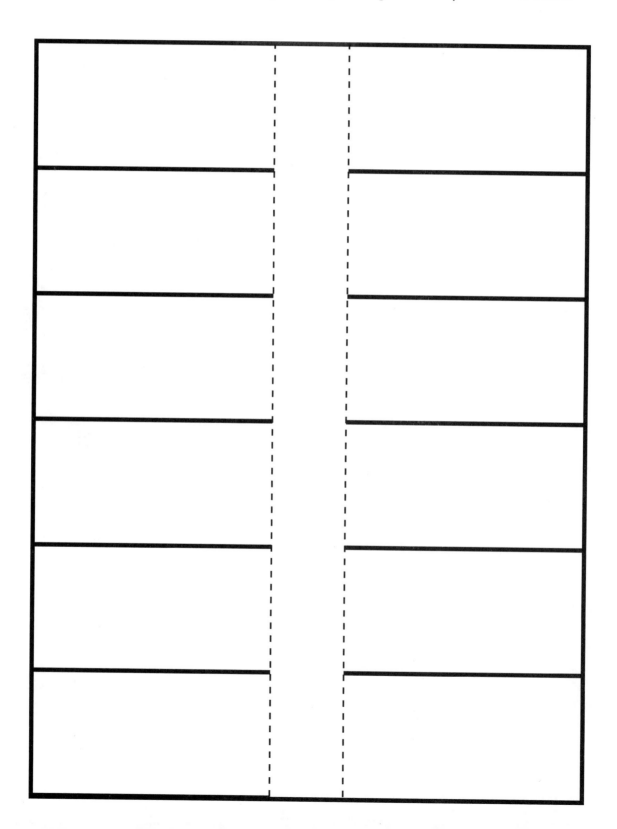

Shaped Flaps

Cut out each shaped flap. Apply glue to the back of the narrow section to attach it to a notebook page.

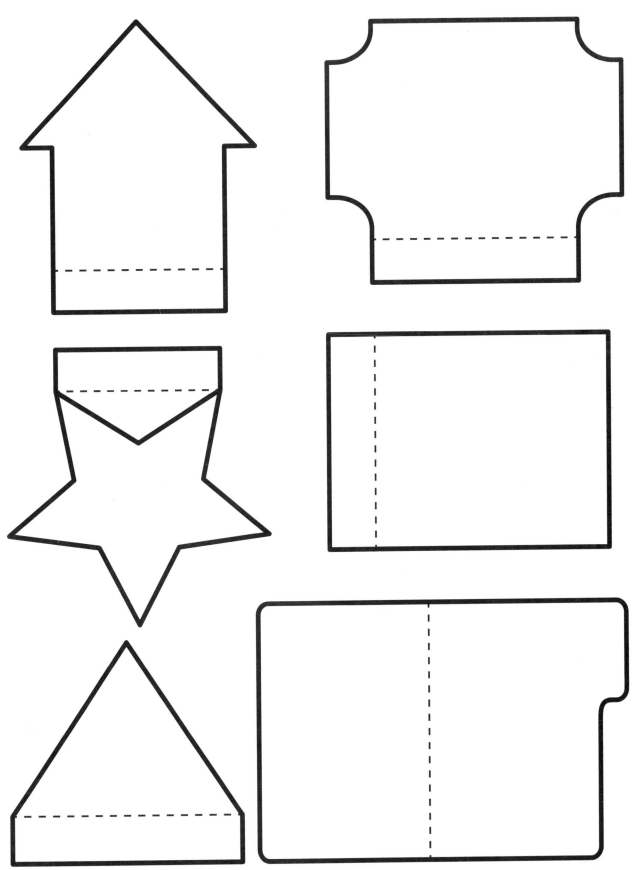

Shaped Flaps

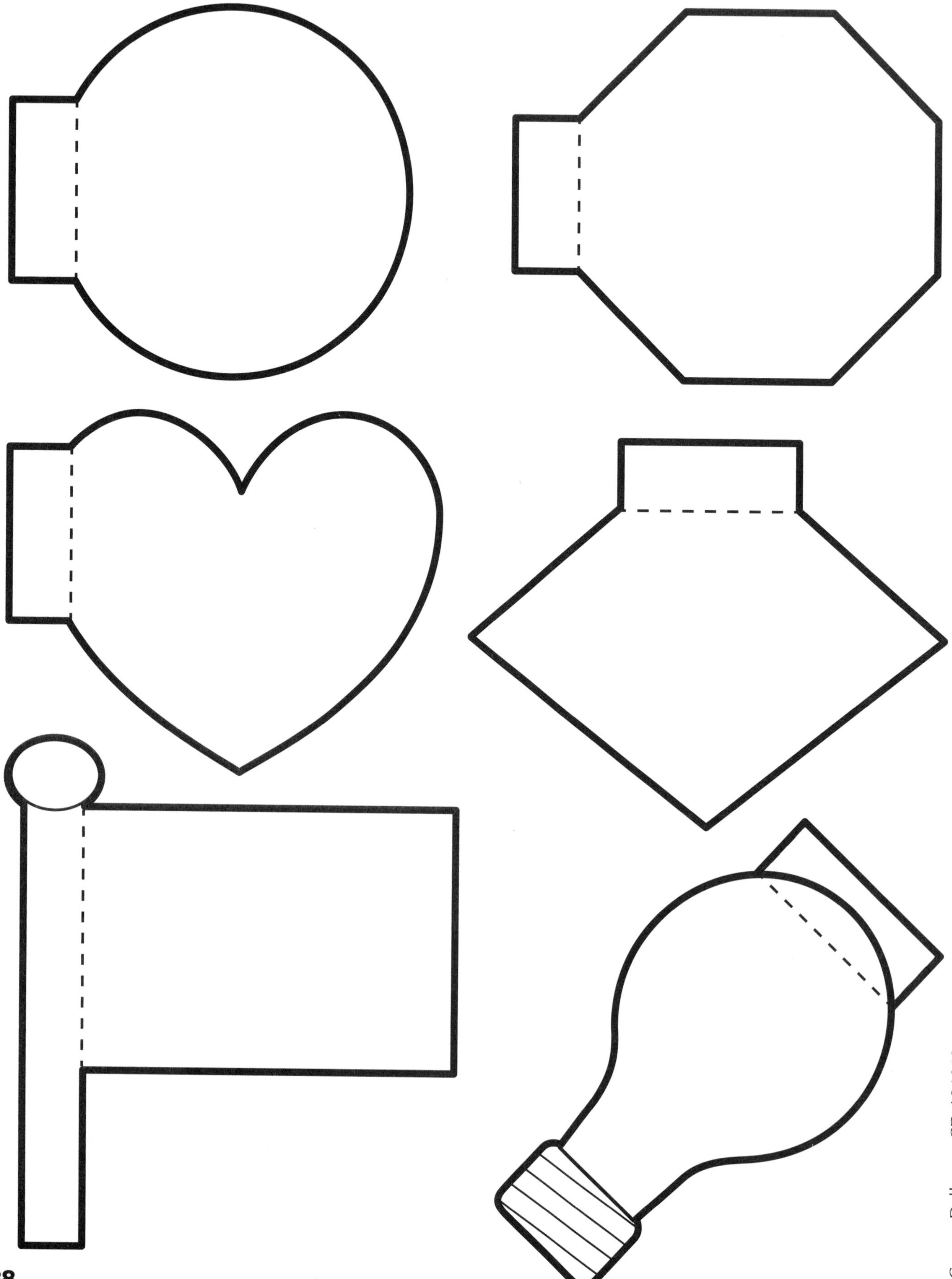

Interlocking Booklet

Cut out the booklet on the solid lines, including the short vertical lines on the top and bottom flaps. Then, fold the top and bottom flaps toward the center, interlocking them using the small vertical cuts. Apply glue to the back of the center panel to attach it to a notebook page.

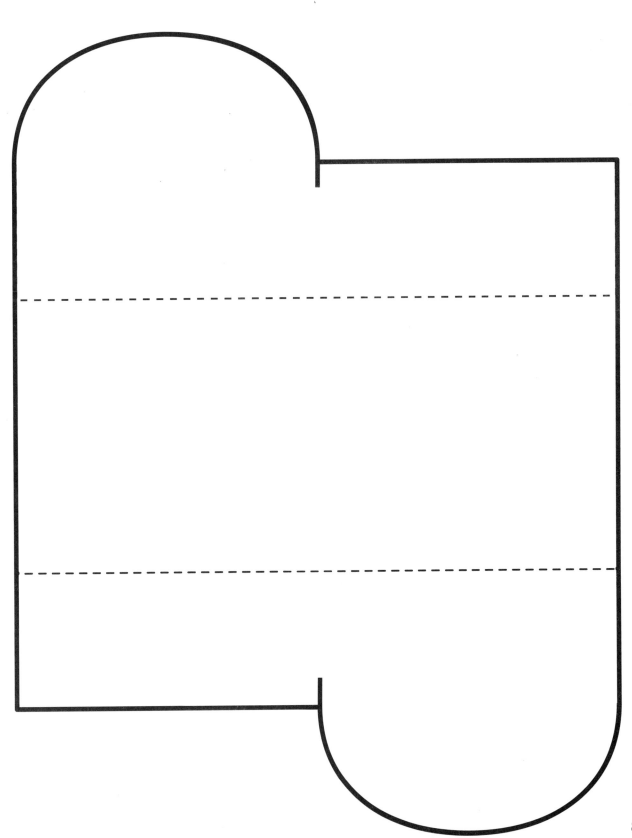

Four-Flap Petal Fold

Cut out the shape on the solid lines. Then, fold the flaps toward the center. Apply glue to the back of the center panel to attach it to a notebook page.

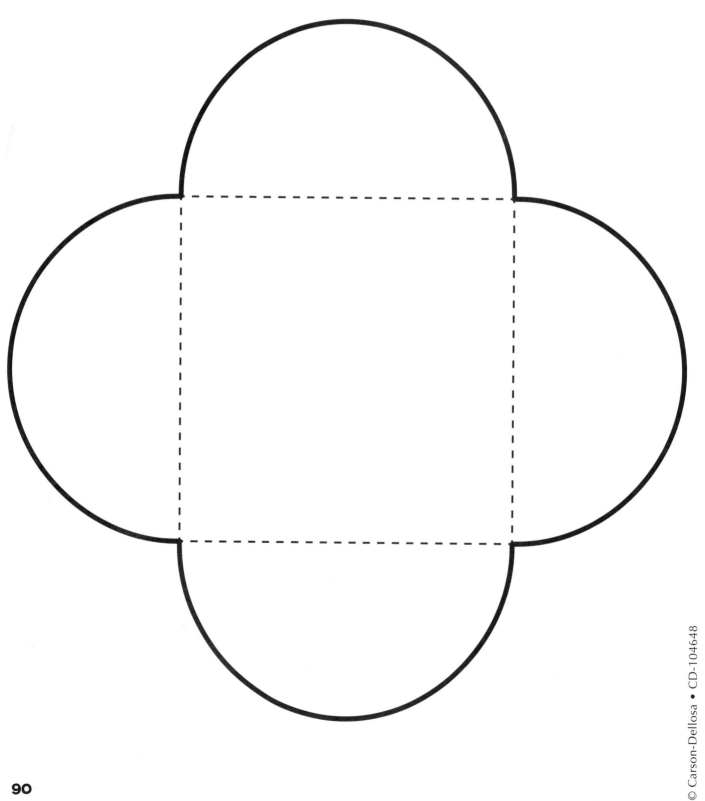

Cut out the shape on the solid lines. Then, fold the flaps toward the center and back out. Apply glue to the back of the center panel to attach it to a notebook page.

Accordion Folds

Cut out the accordion pieces on the solid lines. Fold on the dashed lines, alternating the fold direction. Apply glue to the back of the last section to attach it to a notebook page.

You may modify the accordion books to have more or fewer pages by cutting off extra pages or by having students glue the first and last panels of two accordion books together.

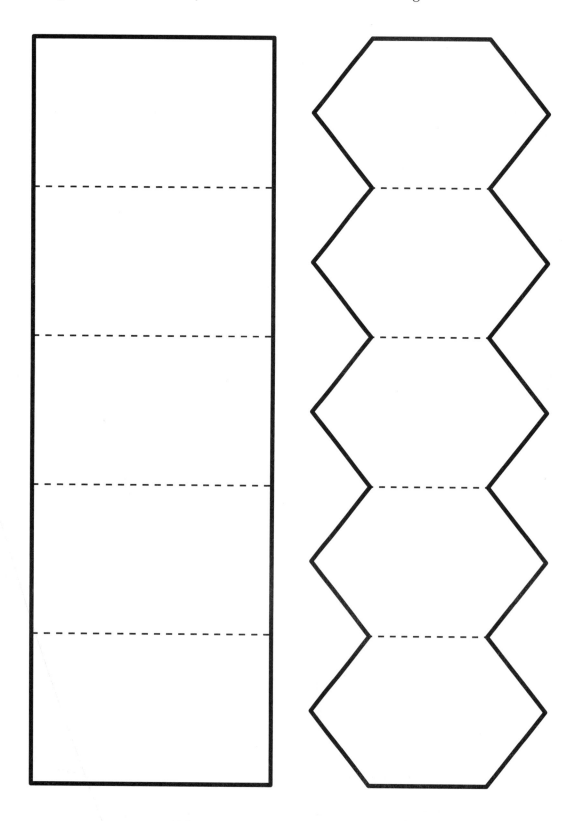

Accordion Folds

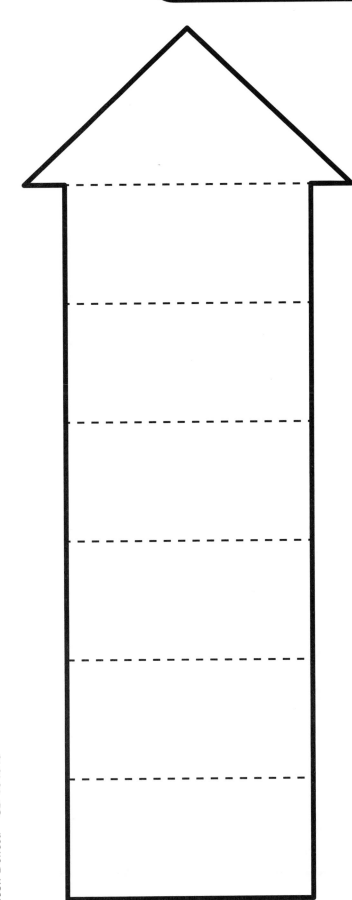

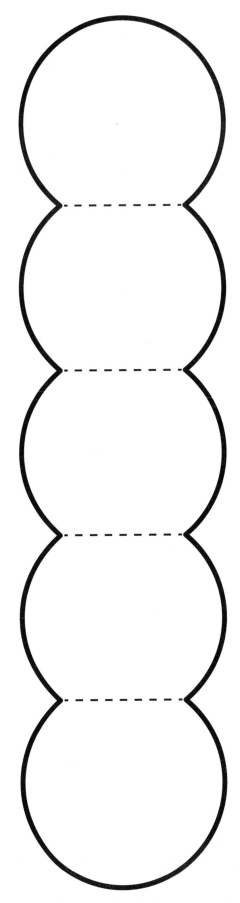

Clamshell Fold

Cut out the clamshell fold on the solid lines. Fold and unfold the piece on the three dashed lines. With the piece oriented so that the folds form an X with a horizontal line through it, pull the left and right sides together at the fold line. Then, keeping the sides touching, bring the top edge down to meet the bottom edge. You should be left with a triangular shape that unfolds into a square. Apply glue to the back of the triangle to attach the clamshell to a notebook page.

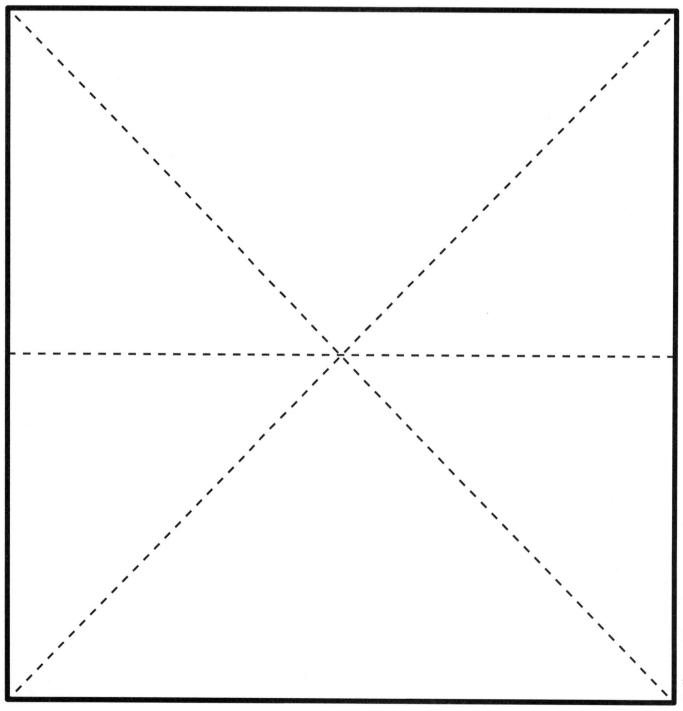

Puzzle Pieces

Cut out each puzzle along the solid lines to create a three- or four-piece puzzle. Apply glue to the back of each puzzle piece to attach it to a notebook page. Alternately, apply glue only to one edge of each piece to create flaps.

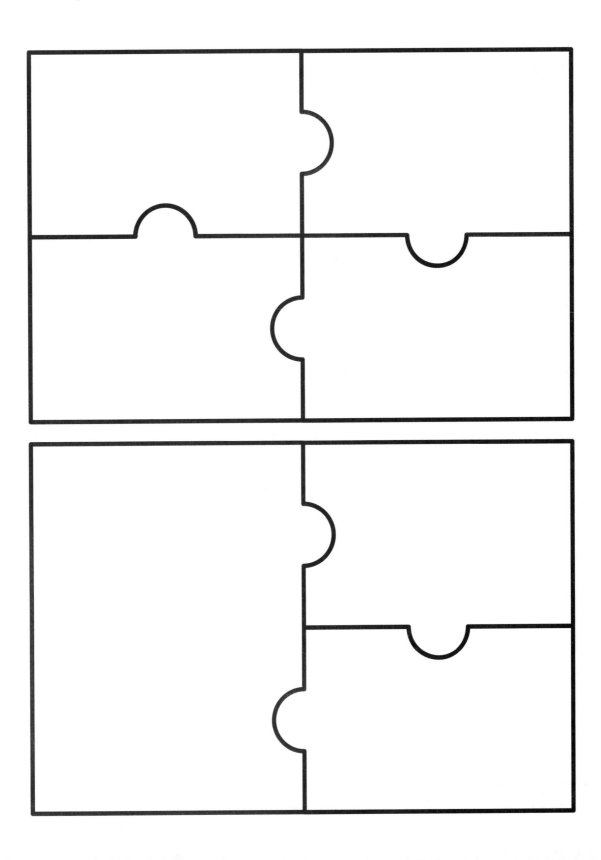

Flip Book

Cut out the two rectangular pieces on the solid lines. Fold each rectangle on the dashed lines. Fold the piece with the gray glue section so that it is inside the fold. Apply glue to the gray glue section and place the other folded rectangle on top so that the folds are nested and create a book with four cascading flaps. Make sure that the inside pages are facing up so that the edges of both pages are visible. Apply glue to the back of the book to attach it to a notebook page.

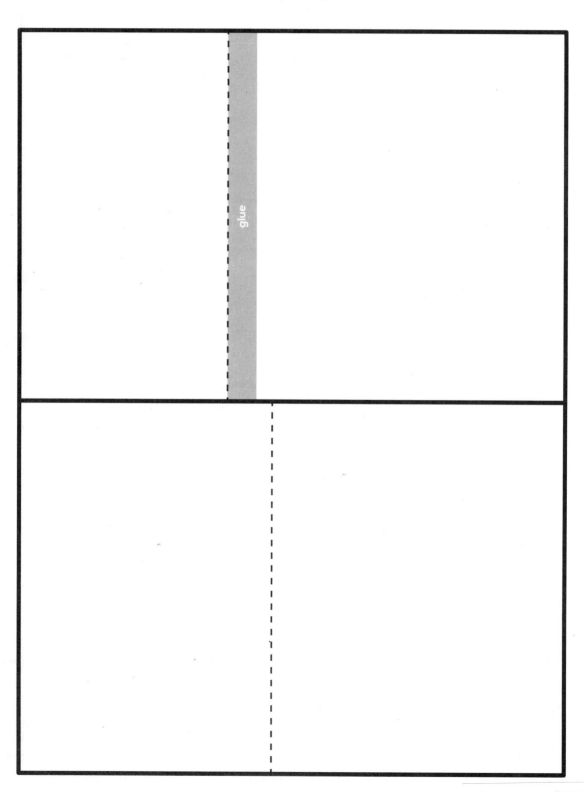

glue